# Imagining Slaves and Robots in Literature, Film, and Popular Culture

D1736715

# Imagining Slaves and Robots in Literature, Film, and Popular Culture

## Reinventing Yesterday's Slave with Tomorrow's Robot

Gregory Jerome Hampton

LEXINGTON BOOKS
Lanham • Boulder • New York • London

Published by Lexington Books
An imprint of The Rowman & Littlefield Publishing Group, Inc.
4501 Forbes Boulevard, Suite 200, Lanham, Maryland 20706
www.rowman.com

Unit A, Whitacre Mews, 26-34 Stannary Street, London SE11 4AB

British Library Cataloguing in Publication Information Available

**Library of Congress Cataloging-in-Publication Data**
The hardback edition of this book was previously catalogued by the Library of Congress as follows:

Hampton, Gregory Jerome, 1968- author.
Imagining slaves and robots in literature, film, and popular culture : reinventing yesterday's slave
with tomorrow's robot / Gregory Jerome Hampton.
pages cm
Includes bibliographical references and index.
1. Technology--Social aspects. 2. Technology in popular culture. 3. Slavery--Social aspects. 4. Slavery in art. 5. Androids--Social aspects. 6. Androids in art. I. Title.
T14.5.H353 2015
303.48'3--dc23
2015027860

ISBN 978-0-7391-9145-3 (cloth : alk. paper)
ISBN 978-1-4985-2758-3 (pbk : alk. paper)
ISBN 978-0-7391-9146-0 (electronic)

Printed in the United States of America

# Contents

# Acknowledgments

The completion of this project is due to the talents, patience, and support of my academic colleagues, friends, and family. I am very grateful for the sporadic and enthusiastic conversation in the hallways with Douglas Taylor. Our conversations about proslavery rhetoric, mythologies of regional difference, and Afro-futurism were both passionate and inspiring. The suggestions made by my office mate, David Green, were invaluable. His erudite perspectives on Hip Hop, Sun Ra, and Janelle Monáe led me down delightful intellectual rabbit holes that I may never emerge from.

Thanks to all of my students, undergraduate and graduate, because they provided me with an audience of critical thinkers and enthusiastic believers in a future that looks very different from the present.

I would also like to thank my wife and children for their moral support and their unwavering ability to keep me grounded by always reminding me of what is most important in life and love.

# Introduction

## Reading the Writing on the Wall

Once upon a time, a great king hosted a great banquet and much wine was consumed. At the banquet praises and thanks were given to the gods of gold, silver, bronze, iron, wood, and stone. The king was pleased with his great city and its impregnable walls and his feast reflected his confidence despite the fact that the city was under siege. The king was proud of all that had been acquired from his enemies and other cities. He was very happy and assured that his reign would see no threats that he would not be able to overcome. The king's city was the greatest city that had ever been created by man and he was its ruler. How frightened the king became when he and his guests watched while the message "Mene, Mene, Tekel Upharsin,"[1] was scribed upon his palace walls. Of course, the king that I am referring to is Belshazzar and his great city was Babylon. I would liken America to the great city of Babylon because there is an impending threat of doom in the mist of greatness and social progress in America. The mysterious hands writing on America's palace walls are mediums of social critique and reflection. Literature, film, music, and popular culture are saturated with messages that caution this nation to move into its future with greater awareness of its past and its potential. It would be a great tragedy if the consumption of much wine and other rhetorical devises were allowed to loll America blindly down a path of self-destruction.

*Imagining Slaves and Robots in Literature, Film, and Popular Culture* is a critical look into the future and the past with regard to the creation of humanoid robots and the historical construction of slave bodies in Antebellum America. This text critiques the relationship between American slaves and humanoid robots of the present and very near future through the reflective lens of literary, film, social, and historical criticism. By examining the construction and employment of slave bodies and their identities in the American literary imagination and considering the roles that humanoid robots have and will play in the future as dictated by science fact and science fiction, this text seeks to question the role of the robot in human society and the cost of such a role. *Imagining Slaves and Robots in Literature, Film, and Popular Culture* is an interdisciplinary meditation that seeks to investigate and speculate about the relationship between technology and human nature. This book is also intended to act as a cautionary devise designed to prevent the fall of another Babylon. Where Belshazzar became over confident of Babylon's material value and technological potential, I would caution America to remember its past employment of the organic technology known as chattel slavery and to consider what happens when desires for gold and silver outweigh the less tangible characteristic of humanity.

This text is unique because it is the first book of criticism that compares antebellum American literature and contemporary science fiction (film and literature) with each other. The idea that antebellum American literature can inform contemporary readers about how robots are being imagined lends a great deal of insight into how race has been employed to mark bodies throughout American history. The notion of identity is at the center of *Imagining Slaves and Robots in Literature, Film, and Popular Culture*, as it necessarily raises question of how race, class, sex, and gender will be integrated with technology and the bodies of the future. Each moment of this meditation is invested in questions dependent upon images of the body and necessarily engages the inextricable issues associated with identifying bodies as dominant and marginalized. In examining the similarities of human slaves and mechanical or biomechanical robots, I hope to gain better understanding of how slaves are created and justified in the imaginations of a supposedly civilized nation. And in doing so, give pause to those who would disassociate America's past from its forming future. In the chapters to follow, I will assert that the enslavement of humans or human-like machines with Artificial Intelligence (AI) or anything resembling an independent consciousness will produce adverse affects among all participants in such an institution. Furthermore, I assert that if and when machines are made to resemble humans in form and deed, there will be an unavoidable miscegenation of machine and humanity that will shift the aesthetic of the human body and the social systems that police human behavior. That which was once defined as inanimate or object, will eventually become animate and possessed of subjectivity despite its man-made origin of being.

Although this discussion may appear to be based on fantastic speculation, its theoretical framing entails literary and historical analysis that will prove to be prophetic in its accuracy. Literary historian Brian Aldiss reminds us that, "all discussions of science fiction involve generalizations" about the real world (Aldiss 14). As a genre, science fiction is unique in its popular conception, but especially in its subject matter. With the appearance of the canonical drama *R. U. R (Rossum's Universal Robots)* in 1921, author and playwright, Karel Capek, forever attached the notion of servitude and African-American experiences to the genre of science fiction. *Imagining Slaves and Robots in Literature, Film, and Popular Culture* is a timely and creative analysis of the ways in which we domesticate technology and the manner in which the history of slavery continues to be utilized in contemporary society. This discussion attempts to inte-

grate, in an interdisciplinary fashion and in language that is easily accessible, the analyses of race and science fiction by juxtaposing a science
fictional artifact with a historical institution.

The goals of this meditation are ambitious even though its length is
brief. In it, I explore a variety of ideas that connect robots to enslaved
Africans in Antebellum America. A predominant premise in this discussion is that robots are becoming the new slaves of the future, in a variety
of ways and this process will likely yield derogatory effects on society as
a whole. Robots, like the enslaved Africans, occupy a liminal status between human and tool. It is the liminal status between human and tool
that will cause the most confusion in society and will act as the catalyst to
redefine and blur identities associated with human and machine. Furthermore, the uses of rhetoric surrounding proslavery arguments are surprisingly similar to those made about robots as domestic servants necessary for the move toward a more productive and technologically advanced civilization. In America's move toward a better version of itself its
technology is bound for the creation of androids with advanced A.I. As
such, there will be similarities to be made between the consciousness of
the robot and the double consciousness of the African-American discussed in the work of W.E. B. Du Bois. It is a goal of this meditation to
consider some of the ramifications of such social and technological shifts
in our society and to better understand why they occur and exactly how
they will change our perceptions of the body and definitions of humanity. And finally, *Imagining Slaves and Robots in Literature, Film, and Popular
Culture* takes on the task of examining how and why the images that are
disseminated among the American populous via film, music, and popular culture all work to normalize the idea of a humanoid robot as a servant and companion. Popular culture has consciously or coincidentally
ensured the American populous that the development of humanoid robots with advanced AI is an inevitable fact that is quickly coming to pass.
Consequently, this text moves to question why robots and slaves seem to
be re-occurring topics in the evolution of human society.

The discussions found in this text are largely dependent on questioned raised in the writing of Isaac Asimov. Asimov was a true scientist
(a professor of biochemistry at the University of Boston) as well as a
major contributor to the literary movement known as the Golden Age of
Science Fiction (1938–1946). Born Isaak Yudovich Ozimov circa 1920 in
Petrovichi, Russia, Asimov was best known for his Foundation series but
was also well know for his Robot series.[2] It is Asimov's depiction of the
robot in his fiction that is most pertinent to this book. As a Jewish/Rus-
sian immigrant, Asimov would have been very familiar with the oppression of marginalized bodies in America as well as abroad. His short stories found in the Robot collection seems to have influenced almost every
depiction the robot in popular culture since 1950. Asimov and Robert
Silverberg expanded the short story "The Bicentennial Man" into a novel

entitled *The Positronic Man*. Issues of slavery, humanity, and race were common topics in both titles. Despite this fact, literary criticism engaging issues of race and robots are not completely common. There is very little scholarship on race and science fiction apart from scattered articles in academic journals such as *Extrapolation, Science-Fiction Studies*, and *The Journal of Utopian Studies*. This text seeks to contribute to the burgeoning but still sparse discourse that critically analyzes racial identity in the genre of science fiction. It begins to fill an absence and facilitate discussions that make direct ties to the slavery experienced by humans and the slavery that might subjugate humans and machines in the future.

One of the most recent publications that critically engages race within the genre of science fiction is *Race in American Science Fiction* (2011). Noting that science fiction is characterized by an investment in the proliferation of racial difference, Isiah Lavender III argues that racial alterity is fundamental to the genre's narrative strategy. *Race in American Science Fiction* offers a systematic classification of ways that race appears and how it is silenced in science fiction, while developing a critical vocabulary designed to focus attention on often-overlooked racial implications. Lavender's focused readings of science fiction contextualize race within the genre's better-known master narratives and agendas. Authors discussed include Isaac Asimov, Ray Bradbury, Philip K. Dick, Octavia Butler, and Ursula K. Le Guin. Lavender's texts supports my assertion that the genre of science fiction is relatively progressive with regards to racial stereotypes propagated by American media and normative culture, but not completely free of racial and racist images of black bodies. Lavender's text attempts to "provide a critical method to encourage and direct attention to long-overlooked racial aspects of science fiction" (Lavender III 19). Like the scholar Toni Morrison, in her *Playing in the Dark*, Lavender III seeks to interrogate the Africanist presence in the traditionally white genre of American science fiction. "Science fiction often talks about race by not talking about race . . ." (Flowers 281). His terms *blackground* and *meta-slavery* acknowledge the ties to African-American experiences as staples for the genre of science fiction.[3] *Imagining Slaves and Robots in Literature, Film, and Popular Culture* steps beyond Lavender's claim that science fiction is not a post-racial genre, and goes further to assert that the genre of science fiction, in the forms of literature, film, and popular culture, is crucial to constructing definitions of race and humanity in the present and future.

Another important text that adds to the discourse of race and science fiction film is *Black Space: Imagining Race in Science Fiction Film* by Adilifu Nama. Nama's text is based on the accurate premise that like literature, film is a direct reflection of the society that produces it. Science fiction film, more often than mainstream film and literature, responds to an audience that is eager to imagine the possibilities of different social structures and identities. Nama is careful to depict how science fiction film recycles images of black bodies as allegories and representations of alien bodies. Through an analysis of canonic science fiction film, Nama demonstrates how American cinema has made a profitable business out of repackaging racist representations of blackness and selling it to the American populous. Nama's text also shows how science fiction film characterizes African Americans and use race as a carrier of meaning" (Kiuchi 272). In *Black Space* American science fiction film, too often, equates otherness with physical and or visual alienness. In many of the examples given, race is a variable of difference that may take on the form of alien, robot, or other. *Black Space* serves *Imagining Slaves and Robots in Literature, Film, and Popular Culture* because it supports the notion that science fiction cinema has become an important field of racial analysis; a site where definitions of race can be contested and re-imagined.

In *Imagining Slaves and Robots in Literature, Film, and Popular Culture* the robot is the lynchpin for the past, present, and future. The robot or slave is a notion that has changed its form over the years but has always been present in the imaginations of evolving human societies. The robot is the one creation of the human imagination that has always been inextricable from the marginalized body and hopes of progress. This contradiction or paradox is crucial in the process of understanding how and why humanity seems so helpless in resisting the temptations of institutional slavery. *Love and Sex with Robots: The Evolution of Human-Robot Relationships* by David Levy is a wide-ranging examination of the emotional and physical relations between humans and the inanimate objects of their desires. In the most straightforward and provocative manner Levy addresses the question of whether or not humans can love robots. Levy answers this question with a resounding affirmative. Levy's text not only asserts that humans will enter into relationships with robots in the future, but cites examples of present-day humans attempting to marry sex-dolls without AI. Levy's approach to a seeming fantastic speculation is both rational and convincing because of his honest and accurate understanding of human sexuality and social behavior. In order to put the reader at ease with the possibility of human-robot love, Levy compares the phenomenon to the ways in which humans fall in love with each other, their pets, and even their motorcycles. From there, Levy argues, it is a short emotional step to the affection people can be expected to display towards robots. Although Levy's topic may initially seem farfetched, his speculation about robot/human relations in the future is founded on sound reasoning. A predominant premise in Levy's discussion is that the human imagination dictates human emotion and reality. If a human chooses to believe a robot can love and feel, that human will inevitably attempt to return or displace those real or imagined feelings of love onto the body of a robot.

One of the most exciting aspects of this project is its attempt to reveal continuities and discontinuities between the past and the very near future based on observations made in the present. The idea that slavery still lingers in the subconscious imaginations of the American populous in such a profound manner that it dictates how undeveloped technology will be employed in the future is profound, and perhaps profoundly frightening. In the first chapter, I attempt to explain why moving into the future without a clear understanding of the past can be dangerous with regards to the development of domestic robots. The impending injection of mechanical robots into mainstream American society is paramount to the implementation of a new form of slavery and the potential restructuring of the American social hierarchy. Through a brief analysis of three classic texts *R. U. R* by Capek, *Clockwork Man* by Odle, and the short story "Robbie" by Isaac Asimov in conjunction with historical readings of the African-American slave experiences and references from contemporary images of robots and technological advancements in the media, I consider the boundaries and lack thereof between American slavery and the employment of robots as a source of slave labor. In this chapter the image of Rosie (the animated robot-maid from *The Jetson's*) is read as propaganda targeting American youth and promoting the acceptance of slave labor as normative. I consider how toys and household appliances are also employed as devises of persuasion and symbols of technological and social progress. The primary function of chapter one is to ponder the possibilities of another form of slavery being reborn in America as a direct result of technological advancement and social conditioning through mass media and the promise of social progress.

Chapter two continues to consider the location of the American family as a primary target for persuasive advertisement designed to normalize notions of slavery in America's past and future. This chapter is a critical examination of the rhetoric that is used in framing the integration of robot technology into the common American household. Chapter two compares the rhetoric used in antebellum proslavery literature to rhetoric used in contemporary speculative fiction and popular culture (film and music). The chapter is invested in the notion that art is a common source of political rhetoric. The texts that will be engaged include the drama "The Benevolent Planter" by Thomas Bellamy; the science fiction short story "Robbie" by Asimov; *Wired for War* by P. W. Singer and various essays from *The Ideology of Slavery: Proslavery Thought in the Antebellum South, 1830–1860*. This chapter seeks to better understand how rhetoric is able to persuade a well-intentioned population to employ immoral institutions when promised a utopian republic.

Chapter three is invested in exploring the boundaries of the human body and its relationship with technology and the robot body. This chapter examines the employment of racial and gender stereotypes in the construction of robots in the American imagination. It attempts to explain how images of the Safire, Jessabelle, and Mammie are distorted and compressed into the gynoid, a sexualized mechanical body. Hazel Carby's

*Reconstructing Womanhood* is used to speculate on the role of female robots and the results of displacing sexual repressed desires onto machines (mechanical bodies) instead of human bodies. Consequently, this chapter seeks to understand why robots and slaves always appear to be imagined as better lovers and companions than their masters and creators.

Chapter four speaks to the inevitable result of master/slave relationships. The tropes of the tragic mulatto and the cyborg are considered as symbols of the evolution of human/machine relations. This chapter seeks to draw significant parallels between Lydia Maria Child's short stories "The Quadroons" (1842) and "Slavery's Pleasant Home" (1843) with more contemporary portrayals of the tragic mulatto found in the films *Imitation of Life* (1934 and 1959) and *Bicentennial Man* (1999). Child was an abolitionist writer, supporter of women's suffrage, the editor and validator of Harriet Jacob's classic feminine slave narrative *Incidents in the Life of a Slave Girl* (1861), and is generally credited as the first writer to feature a tragic mulatto/mulatta in her fiction. This chapter is invested in critically analyzing the origins of the racially ambiguous mulatto and understanding how the cyborg (human/robot hybrid) iterates many of the same desires and fears in the imagination of American popular culture. The phenomenon of *passing* is also examined in this chapter as a natural progression of miscegenation of biology and technology. As the machine becomes indistinguishable from the human, the question of human identity is necessarily placed in a space of ambiguity and the identity of the machine becomes blurred as well.

Chapter five takes up the question of ambiguous identity by looking to past theories of racial identity in twentieth century America. It the question of consciousness that is central to this discussion because it is consciousness and free will that ultimately defines humanity and distinguishes it as animate and alive. This chapter is a meditation on the meaning of racial identity and consciousness as is discussed in W. E. B. Du Bois' first chapter of his *Souls of Black Folk* (1903) in conjunction with the very critical insights presented in the short stories found in Isaac Asimov's collection *I, Robot (1950)*. The notion of double consciousness and Cartesian thought seem to intersect when Du Bois' Negro American begins to question his/her place in white America. Likewise, when Asimov's robots begin to question their roles within human society AI produces a paradox that blurs the borders of mechanical and biological. This chapter attempts to better understand the similarities that might be shared among all marginalized characters; human, mechanical, or hybrid and what such identities might come to mean in the defining of a national identity.

Chapter six focuses on images of the robot in contemporary popular culture. This chapter begins with a critique of one of the oldest portrayals of the robot in cinema. The silent black and white German made film *Metropolis* is discussed as the source material for the African-American

Hip-Hop artist Janelle Monáe. The German made silent film was written and directed by Fritz Lang and his wife, Thea von Harbou, and depicts the creation and employment of a robot as a device designed to manipulate and eventually replace the proletariat. Consequently, *Metropolis* is read as a Marxist cautionary tale for the arrival of singularity. Monáe, however, uses the film as inspiration for her musical album *ArchAndroid*, a collection of politically charged songs designed to fight the notion of slavery and marginalization in general. Monáe's successful and lucrative employment of the android persona (Cindi Mayweather) suggests that the image of the domestic robot has been embraced by mainstream society as a plausible notion. Furthermore, the plight of oppression experienced by such characters has already been reduced to mundane entertainment surrounded by singing and dancing.

My motivation for developing this project is partially due to my interpretation of Asimov's short stories and novels about robots and the uncanny likeness that I see when considering the condition of the African-American slave and the condition of mechanical robots in Asimov's fictional future. I say *partially* because my other motivating factor was, in many regards, due to the random viewing of a YouTube video that included four backup singers and a lead singer performing for a presumably Asian audience.[4] The singers sang in Japanese and all five performers shared the appearance of agile and attractive Asian females. Upon closer examination it became evident that the lead singer was a humanoid robot designed to look, sound, and move like a human performing on stage. Consequently my interests were peaked and my research ensued. Questioning ones' identity usually begins in front of a mirror. When the image in the mirror does not coincide with the image in the imagination it is time to reconsider our definitions of reality. The technological developments in our world are beginning to ask that we become more aware of the movement of the world surrounding us. Discussions of singularity, the production of domestic robots, and the insatiable desire to develop advanced AI may be equivalent to King Belshazzar's writing on the wall.

This book attempts to address issues that are crucial in the process of understanding what the future of the Western world will look like as we approach the adolescents of the twenty-first century. By drawing parallels between antebellum American literature, contemporary science fiction literature and film, and the present-day market place of popular culture, the bodies of tomorrow are revealed. This book asks its readers to consider how far humanity will go in order to create a utopian-like republic. It also begs the question of how many times America will lie to itself about its past dependency on institutions of slavery and its immoral and immature addiction to materialism.

## NOTES

1. Once when King Belshazzar was banqueting with his lords and drinking wine from the golden vessels of the Temple of Yahweh, a man's hand was seen writing on the wall certain mysterious words. Frightened by the apparition, the king ordered his astrologers to explain the inscription; but they were unable to read it. Daniel was then summoned to the royal palace; and the king promised him costly presents if he would decipher the inscription. Daniel read it "Mene, mene, tekel, upharsin" and explained it to mean that God had "numbered" the kingdom of Belshazzar and brought it to an end; that the king had been weighed and found wanting; and that his kingdom was divided and given to the Medes and Persians (Dan. v. 1–28).

2. Details of Asimov's life can be found in his memoir. *I Asimov: A Memoir*. New York: Random House, 2009.

3. Lavender III "introduces the reader to the *background* of science fiction, a concept that refers to the unspoken racial assumptions that underlie the history of SF writing. Other terms in Lavender's book include *meta-slavery* (the trope of performing the history of African American slavery on other worlds and in other times)" (Fawaz 201).

4. See Japanese Robot Pop Star video on YouTube posted October 28, 2010. www.youtube.com/watch?v=8LXACLbfRKs.

## REFERENCES

Aldiss, Brian W. *Trillion Year Spree: The History of Science Fiction*. New York: Avon Books, 1986.

Fawaz, Ramzi. Book Review. "Super Black: American Pop culture and Black Superheroes/Do the Gods Wear Capes? Spirituality, Fantasy, and Superheroes/ Race in American Science Fiction." *American Literature*. Mar 2013, Vol. 85 Issue 1, p. 199–202.

Flowers, Tiffany A. Book Review. "Race in American Science Fiction." *Western Journal of Black Studies*. Winter 2014, Vol. 38 Issue 4, p. 281–282.

Kiuchi, Yuya. Book Review. "Black Space: Imagining Race in Science Fiction Film by Adilifu Nama." *Journal of American Culture*. Sept 2009, Vol. 32 Issue 3, p. 271–272.

Monaco, James. *How to Read a Film: Movies Media and Beyond*. New York: Oxford University Press, 2009.

# ONE

# Racing Robots and Making Slaves

*How the Past Informs the Future*

With the technological advances over the past few decades it is inevitable that the creation and dissemination of robots and similar technology will become commonplace in the households and imaginations of the American populous. Lev Grossman's *Time Magazine* article, "Singularity-2045: The Year Man Becomes Immortal," comments on Raymond Kurzweil's speculations about the inevitable invent of AI (Artificial Intelligence) and its influence on humanity. Grossman and Kurzweil agree that the possibilities of the future are now realities quickly coming to pass, as technological advances are occurring exponentially without any signs of slowing. The future is upon us; the only question that remains is how we are going to respond to it. The fact that millions of Americans are walking around right now with "smart" cell phones called Droids (short for Androids) only begins to hint at what is to come. Japan has already produced humanoid robots that can sing, dance, and assist with various household duties. In the year 2000 Japan's automotive company Honda introduced the world to one of the most advanced humanoid domestic robots to date, ASIMO (an acronym for Advanced Step Innovative Mobility).[1] The term "domestic robot" is in itself a fascinating and complicated notion considering the etymology behind the soon-to-be normative phrase. The term "robot" in Czech means slave or compulsory labor (Nakamura 172). Of course the English term "domestic" refers to the domicile or house. Although the terms "domestic robot" and "house slave" may initially appear to be unrelated, they are in actuality synonymous when one begins to interrogate the truth of American history and destiny.

1

Slavery, after all, was largely invested in producing and controlling a labor force, which was dissociated from humanity. In many regards American slavery was a failed experiment to employ flesh and blood machines as household appliances, farm equipment, sex toys, and various tools of industry without the benefits of human and civil rights. Consequently, what is interesting about the production and development of mechanical robots is how they are being assigned both race and gender as identity markers. Why does a machine need such a complex identity, if that machine is designed to only complete the mundane labor that humanity wishes to forego? One plausible response is that the robot is being designed to be more than an appliance but less than a human. The technology of the twenty-first century is in the process of developing a modern day socially accepted slave.

Literature has always been a direct reflection of the society that produces it and acts as an excellent tool for forecasting any societal shifts that may occur. The presence of the word robot in literature can be dated back as far as 1921. Karel Capek's play R. U. R. (Rossum's Universal Robot) produced in Czechoslovakia was not merely a science fictive fantasy; it was a prophetic look into humanity's destiny. The employment of the robot remains at the center of the literary genre of science fiction and is inextricable from the discourse of slavery and the African American. Unfortunately, if such a machine happens to take root in the American social system, which was founded on the notion of slavery, the results will yield an abysmal circumstance of hierarchy. This chapter will consider the boundaries and borders that occur in the evolving discourse of robots and slaves.

Brian Calvert's article "Slavery in Plato's Republic" engages the debate to whether or not Plato's utopian society contained slaves. In his discussion he considers how Plato's student, Aristotle, interpreted the slave as an animate tool. Calvert notes that in Book I of *Politics* by Aristotle that,

> Aristotle tells us that the natural slave does not possess reason, that he is useful, like a domestic animal, for the provision of the necessities of life by bodily service, and that nature intends to make the body of the natural slave different from that of the freeman. The body of the slave ought to be suited for heavy labor. (Calvert 368)

Calvert concludes his discussion of slavery in Plato's Republic with a very clear assertion that slavery and the slave would have no place in Plato's utopian society. Furthermore, the slave and slavery would be antithetical to a Republic that is dependent upon reasonable citizens who are employed by their own labors and studies of art and philosophy. Aristotle, unlike his teacher, Plato, has very clear views of the role of the slave in a society, as demonstrated in the above passage. Aristotle defined the slave as a human being who by nature (God) does not belong to himself but to another person. Such a person is imagined as property or an animate tool needed to support the life of its owner.[2] To image a machine in the place of a flesh and blood human is not a difficult task when considering Aristotle's definition of slave. It is not difficult to see how a dark brown body with foreign phenotype, and foreign tongue might be mistaken for a slave as defined by Aristotle; absent of reason and naturally different from a white freeman. Unfortunately, the definitions of the past continue to influence how society imagines the bodies of the future.

Capek's motivation for his play *R. U. R.* was partly World War One (WWI) the "greatest and bloodiest war the world had seen, a war featuring all the inventions of modern science and technology, bombs, poison gas, machine guns, airplanes, and tanks" (Capek ix). Capek's play symbolized a loss of hope for the future of humanity. WWI shattered "the commonly shared illusion that by means of unprecedented technical progress, civilization was moving toward a better, easier life" (Capek ix). This societal shift has historically been referred to as modernism and it is the failings of humanity at the cusp of such great potential that makes Capek's drama so continuously relevant. I assert that with *R. U. R.*, Capek rewrites the narrative of American slavery fifty-six years after its legal abolition as a cautionary tale that speaks to the technologically advancing nations of the world.

The impending injection of mechanical robots into mainstream American society is paramount to the implementation of a new form of slavery and the potential restructuring of the American social hierarchy. Through a brief analysis of three classic texts *R. U. R* by Capek, *Clockwork Man* by Odle, and the short story "Robbie" by Isaac Asimov in conjunction with historical readings of the African-American slave experiences and references from contemporary speculation about robots and technological advancements, I will consider the boundaries and lack thereof between American slavery and the employment of robots as a source of slave labor. To be clear, the predominant premise of my discussion is that the transatlantic slave trade and the employment of chattel slavery can be interpreted as the invention that allowed America to establish its social and economic status in the world. Within this discussion I also wish to ponder the possibilities of another form of slavery being reborn in America as a direct result of technological capabilities to produce human doppelgangers.

Not surprisingly, most of the scholarship addressing robots and the notion of slavery in literature fall under the category of science fiction literary criticism. The idea of examining the creation of robots in the real world as a form of neo-slavery has not been considered seriously in Western letters. Japan, however, has been pondering the influences of such technology on human social systems since the turn of the twentieth century. Since *R. U. R.*'s translation into Japanese in 1923, "Japan witnessed a boom of literature about robots (*jinzo ningen*)" (Nakamura 169). This boom in conjunction with a rise in industrialization and mechanization contributed greatly to Japan's modernist movement in literature and art (170). In "Marking bodily difference: mechanized bodies in Hirabayashi Hatsunosuke's 'Robot' and early Showa robot literature," Miri Nakamura explains how Japanese modernism (*modanizumu*) is a "complicated movement that attempts to capture the spirit of the current epoch and its trends in literature and the arts, defining itself against more traditional and orthodox forms" (175). During this movement in Japan the notion of the robot was considered as potentially being something more complicated than a convenient tool, obedient pet or loyal slave. In Japanese literature dating back as early as the 1920s, the robot has been thought of as a potential threat to biological humans due to their inevitable evolution toward human likeness. The possibility of a robot *passing* as a human was one of the most frightening and threatening aspects of such a technological advancement. This is clearly reminiscent of the threat of the mulatto in the Americas. There is a great deal of African American fiction as well as literary criticism and theory dedicated to the notion of "passing" and most of it has evolved from slave experience(s).[3]

Li Gong's article "The boundary of racial prejudice: Comparing preferences for computer-synthesized White, Black, and robot characters," "presents alarming strength of racial prejudice and cast doubt on the notion of all-human in-group favoritism in comparison to robots" (Gong 2074). If and when robots are integrated into mainstream society the mythology that humanity will forego its petty racial hierarchies and unite on grounds of human solidarity is unlikely; racism appears to be a permanent fixture in and among human social systems.[4] Whether this is surprising or not, what is at least interesting is the fact that race is believed to be a major factor in the production of machines. Gong's research reinforces the notion that the anonymity that the internet has created does not preclude the practice of marking bodies found in the real world; race matters even where it should not. In many respects race acts as a sort of seasoning for the body that allows it to be digested or understood by various social systems. Consequently, a body without race can only be imagined as alien, if it can be imagined at all.

Whether a marker on metal or synthetic skin, race gives a body position in the social hierarchy. By assigning race to robots, the robot is admitted into the *space of potential humanity*. The slaves of Antebellum America were initially easily identifiable. Initially the appearance of the African slave was distinct in pigmentation and phenotype. Thus, the assignment of a racial designation for the African located at the bottom of the social hierarchy required less effort than marking a less physically distinct European body.[5] However, by including the slave in the social hierarchy at all, moved them within the boundaries of humanity at least in the imaginations of the slave holding class. Frederick Douglass addressed such phenomenon in his famous slave narrative.

> Every year brings with it multitudes of this class of slaves. It was doubtless in consequence of knowledge of this fact, that one great statesman of the south predicted the downfall of slavery by the inevitable laws of population. If the lineal descendants of Ham are alone to be scripturally enslaved, it is certain that slavery at the south must soon become unscriptural; for thousands are ushered into the world, annually, who, like myself, owe their existence to white fathers, and those fathers most frequently their own masters. (Douglass 44)

As a result of miscegenation (an inevitable law of population) the slaves' distinct appearance became less distinct and allowed some slaves to *pass* as members of the master class. To be clear, miscegenation affected the slave body externally as well as internally. That is to say that the slave body was transformed biologically as well as culturally. The slave was allowed or forced to learn the master's language and culture as a necessary means of survival. Consequently, the black African slave was transformed into a biological and cultural hybrid (African-American) possessed with all of the master's tools to define humanity. And as miscegenation is rarely one-sided, the slave master was also mutated culturally, if not biologically, in the process of absorbing the African slave into a Western social system. The African slave was redesigned and reprogrammed as a result of racial, social, and cultural miscegenation.

## Robot Narrative Form and Function

The traditional masculine slave narrative takes the form of a first person account intending to persuade sympathetic white northern readers to abolish the American institution of slavery. The narrative borrows its methodology and form from popular literary genres of the period—autobiography, biblical texts, epic poetry, and the sentimental novel. The slave narrative like the genres that it reflects is dependent upon romantic methods of persuasion for its success. That is to say, as an example of American romanticism the slave narrative is depended upon persuading its readers through rhetorical devices that primarily target the emotions of a reader, pathos. To be sure, ethos (ethics) and logos (logic) are also adroitly applied to convince its audience of the morally corrupt and spiritually damning nature of slavery. However, what is too often overlooked by twenty-first century readers, (mainly students) is that such an argument suggests the fantastic. Slave narratives were about the business of selling the idea that chattel (cows, chickens, horses, and beasts of burden) that could read, write, and have souls. No wonder the target of persuasion was emotion instead of rational thought, statics, facts, and scientific evidence. No wonder such narratives promised the reward of virtue if the readers shed tears for the humanoid beast of burden stuck in bondage. How else could the population of a new nation be led to believe that the foundation of its economy and social hierarchy was tragically doomed despite its wealth and prosperity? In short, the autobiography of the slave was pseudo-science fiction/fantasy. No wonder the slave narrative's primary target was young white women, slaves themselves to the brain-washing doctrines of the cult of true womanhood or the four cardinal virtues (the laws of a virtuous woman). Antebellum America was ripe for the notion of the robot as any new nation in the demand for cheap/ free labor would be.

Like the Four Cardinal Virtues, the Three Laws of Robotics are a set of rules designed to maintain order. Devised by Isaac Asimov (critic, author, and scientist) the rules were introduced in his 1942 short story "Runaround." The Three Laws are:

1. A robot may not injure a human being or, through inaction, allow a human being to come to harm.
2. A robot must obey the orders given to it by human beings, except where such orders would conflict with the First Law.
3. A robot must protect its own existence as long as such protection does not conflict with the First or Second Laws. (Asimov 37)

In *Reconstructing Womanhood*, Hazel Carby speaks of the four cardinal virtues of womanhood as the laws that enslaved any white woman wishing to be deemed virtuous that is valued by the land owning white male population. "The attributes of True Womanhood, by which a woman judged herself and was judged by her husband, her neighbors and society, could be divided into four cardinal virtues—piety, purity, submissiveness and domesticity . . . with them she was promised happiness and power" (Carby 23). The virtues primarily acted as an ideal code of ethics by defining borders of behavior as well as identity. It was of paramount importance for the master class to control all of the female bodies on the plantation as the social hierarchy was dependent upon a distinct racial/ biological divide largely defined by the production of bodies via the women on the plantation.

> Without the oppression of *all* women, the planter class could not be assured of absolute authority. In a biracial slave society where "racial purity" was a defining characteristic of the master class, total control of the reproductive females was of paramount concern for elite males. Patriarchy was the bedrock upon which the slave society was founded, and slavery exaggerated the pattern of subjugation that patriarchy had established. (Carby 24)

The condition of a slave was dependent on the condition the mother. If the mother of a child was defined as a slave, then that child would also be defined as a slave. Conversely, if a child was born of a free mother, that child would be free and potentially subject to become a member of the land owning class. Such a phenomenon would disrupt the social hierarchy of the slave plantation household.

On a very fundamental level Asimov's laws of robotics are identical to the laws of slavery (for white women as well as black slaves). What is most interesting about such laws is the necessity of their existence. That is to say, the mere fact that slaves or mechanical appliances would warrant a need for codes of conduct suggests a level of reason that seems antithetical to the definition of a slave or appliance. Rational thought suggests that chickens and lawn mowers do not need laws to dictate their behavior and to curve their desires to runs amuck in the yard. The term *desire* does not exist where there is no soul or consciousness. The character Hallemeier (head of the institute for robot psychology) in *R. U. R* tells Helena Glory (the only human female protagonist in the play) that, "they [robots/slaves] have no will of their own, no passion, no history, no soul. Robots love nothing, not even themselves" (Capek 19). One might then say that the laws are for the owners and masters of chattel and appliance. However, this line of thinking suggests that owners and masters are subject to misemploy their property in fashions that might become detrimental to the greater slave holding society. At this speculative juncture it becomes evident that any form of slavery is just as harmful to the master as it is to the slave. This theory has been demonstrated vividly in most canonical slave narratives but has also been employed by more contemporary narratives involving slave/master relations.

*Metal Mammies and Uncle Toms*

Asimov's short story "Robbie" was first published under the title of "Strange Playfellow" in the September 1940 issue of *Super-Science Stories.* The story was about a robot nursemaid who is loved by the child it is assigned to care for yet feared and despised by the mother of the child, Gloria. "Robbie" was Asimov's first robot story and as such, it is one of the purest imaginings of the mechanical robot in the genre of science fiction. Gloria's mother, Mrs. Weston, refers to Robbie as a "terrible machine" (Asimov 7). Mrs. Weston's derogatory description of Robbie can too easily be replaced with the Antebellum term *Bad Nigga*, which carries the same level of malevolence intended for any field or house slave. Despite this declaration, it is made clear by Gloria's father, George Weston, that Robbie is an expensive commodity. "[H]e certainly isn't a terrible machine. He's the best darn robot money can buy and I'm damned sure he set me back half a year's income. He's worth it, though—darn sight cleverer than half my office staff" (Asimov 7). Robbie is male gendered by *his* name and his designation by Gloria's family but his performance is very similar to that of a female domestic servant. Although

Robbie's *skin* is metallic, he is written as a person of color as evidenced by Mrs. Weston's treatment of Robbie.

As there is no mention of Gloria's racial identity, it can be safely assumed that she and her family are white and wealthy.[6] Robbie does the work of a domestic robot but is written as an antebellum Mammy or Uncle Tom willing to risk life and limb for the *masters'* children in the big house. Even after being sold away from Gloria, Robbie remains devoted to little Ms. Gloria as demonstrated by his rescue of her in a factory in New York City. Robbie's rescue of Gloria is especially symbolic because of the location of the incident in a factory. Although Robbie was designed to be a domestic robot/house slave, George Weston has "engineered" (Asimov 22) Gloria's reunion with Robbie in a location more appropriate for an assembly line construction robot or field slave. In the case of Robbie, a construction factory is equivalent to a cotton or sugarcane field. Mrs. Weston uncovers Mr. Weston's ruse when she states, "Robbie wasn't designed for engineering or construction work. He couldn't be of any use to them. You had him placed there deliberately so that Gloria would find him. You know you did" (22). The short story "Robbie" seems to suggest an unavoidable similarity to Antebellum America. If robots are employed as they have been imaged, as marginalized characters, the resurrection of a slave community will inevitably ensue.

In *R. U. R.* humanity's downfall is largely blamed on the act of giving the robots souls. Helena convinces Dr. Gall (head of the physiological and research divisions of R. U. R) to make the Robots more human than humans by giving them the ability to develop souls. This transformation is easily reminiscent of Kurzweil's theories of AI and its ability to allow machines to think and reason for themselves. In Japanese modernist literature "this overturns the power hierarchy. They [robots] become imagined as beings that no longer require their human counterparts and transcend human reach and power" (Nakamura 177).

In his *Discourse on the Origin of Inequality* the French philosopher, Jean-Jacques Rousseau, suggests that perhaps it is not about misemployment, but about a twisted fate of sorts.

> . . . Since all the progress of the human species continually moves away from its primitive state, the more we accumulate new knowledge, the more we deprive ourselves of the means of acquiring the most important knowledge of all. Thus, in a sense, it is by dint of studying man that we have rendered ourselves incapable of knowing him. (Rousseau 113)

Rousseau seems to be suggesting that the more knowledge humanity is exposed to or acquires, the more it develops an inability to understand itself. After coming to an understanding of mathematics, physics, and movement in addition to the technological development of certain tools/ weapons humanity becomes lazy and blinded. Too often, we would rather send a text message rather than engage in face-to-face conversation. The intimate act of writing and mailing a handwritten letter to a loved one has been replaced with a truncated gesture of sending an e-mail (electronic mail). Rousseau warns us that by investing too much in the creations of humanity we may lose sight of our definition of humanity. The assumption that humanity understands itself well enough to reproduce a likeness of itself with its technology is plausible as well as potentially detrimental. If humanity is intelligent enough to create a machine that does the work it would have to do otherwise, it will undoubted create such a machine even at the cost of its own human identity. Thus, it becomes evident that Karel Capek's play R. U. R. was not merely a science fictive fantasy; it was a prophetic look into humanity's future. The engineers and scientists in Capek's play have lost sight of what is truly valuable about humanity. They have allowed their hubris and intellect to lead them down a path of self-destruction.

*What Real Men Do*

In "Robots, Clones and Clockwork Men: The Post-Human Perplex in early Twentieth-Century Literature and Science," Patrick Parrinder examines E. V. Odle's *Clockwork Man* with the intent to consider how the robot and the human body was imagined in the early twentieth century as compared to the cyborg/android post-human body of contemporary science fictive literary traditions. In short, an android is a "replacement or substitute human being" where the *cyborg* is a "man-machine hybrid" (Parrinder 60). The android or humanoid robot is most analogous to the African slave in America, where the cyborg is something more analogous to the result of the inevitable miscegenation that occurs when biology intersects with technology.[7] Odle's *Clockwork Man* is the story of sexless man-made cyborg from the year 8000. Due to a malfunction with its mechanical brain, it is transported back in time to the year 1923 during a cricket game in an English country village. As Clockwork Man (CWM) is initially thought to be just an odd character with a wig it can safely be assumed that it was understood to be of the Caucasian persuasion, as no mention of race was made in the novel.[8] As Parrinder notes "the local doctor thinks [CWM to be] 'the realization of the future,' 'the supreme marvel of human ingenuity' and an embodiment of scientific prophecies of future evolution—in effect, he is the future human being of the To-day and To-morrow series made flesh" (Odle). Odle's *Clockwork Man* is in no way as engaging as Capek's drama or most contemporary robot narratives, however, it is valuable because it renders a fairly vivid picture of how some people imagined humanity in the future. What is most interesting in this image of the future is the continued role of reproduction.

CWM is sexless and as a result does not have the physical ability to reproduce. Capek's robots are faced with the same obstacle. Rossum's robots are "of normal human height and respectable human shape" (Ca-pek 9). After twenty years the robots don't die, they are designed to simply wear out. It is also important to note that Rossum's robots are made from a special "batter" mixed in vats large enough the produce "a thousand Robots at a time" (13). In *R. U. R.* the robot is created with the purpose of providing "the cheapest labor" (Capek 3). Harry Domin (cen-tral director of Rossum's Universal Robots) stairs at a poster in his office that reads "New—Tropical Robots—$150." "Buy Your Very Own Robot." "Looking to Cut Production Costs? Order Rossum's Robots." It is evident that economics played a large role in the production of the robots in Capek's drama. As with American slavery the labor force has always been inextricable from the production of goods and wealth. Unfortunate-ly, the desire to have "human" relationships or interactions with the la-bor force often gets in the way of production.

The desire to interact with robots is what will lead to the rise and fall of a robotic age. Contemporary scientists and engineers assert that believ-able robot characters are important in human-robot interaction. In the article "Believable Robot Characters" scientist and engineers "contend that believable characters evoke users' social responses that, for some tasks, lead to more natural interactions and are associated with improved task performance" (Capek 39). If humans can imagine the machines they are employing as human or at least similar to themselves, the level of human-robot productivity, possibly (re)productivity, is likely to be great-er. For this same group, *believable* means an illusion of life. Too often the illusion of life is eventually equated with the reality of life. This is the work of literature. This is the work of science fiction.

### Real Life in the Cartoons

In a *Times Magazine* article published in 1988, "A Day in the Life: A Family of Four and Their Robots, 25 Years From Now," Nicole Yorkin makes some fairly accurate speculations about the city of Los Angeles in the year 2013. Yorkin predicts the popularity of CD and DVD players, smaller fuel-efficient cars, automated kitchen appliances, and the smart phones along with several other technological advances that have come to pass since 1988. She quotes Behnam Bavarian, the director of UC Ir-vine's Robotics Research Lab as saying, "The robot will be a reality in 25 years. They'll be the next technology item made for households after the PC" (Yorkin 18). Although robots are indeed a reality in present day, they have not become popular or affordable enough to be considered house-hold appliances.[9] Yorkin's article correctly suggests that the robot has been defined as a normative concept, if only in the imagination of the American populous. The media is working hard to instill the idea that a robot is something that can be useful and affordable. Robots can be sent to Mars; they can assist the elderly; they can build automobiles; they can even assist in fighting wars, but the robot in its humanoid form has not yet been broadly accepted as a viable concept in anyplace other than television and the silver screen. It would seem that Astro the Dog is more acceptable in our Western homes than Rosie the outdated and slightly bulky the domestic servant.[10] In fact, for about $150 a family can purchase a robotic dog, Zoomer, right now. Zoomer is a toy produced in China and is described as playful, funny, and likely to steal your heart shortly after being removed from its box. Zoomer can be trained/programmed to do all the tricks a real dog is expected to perform without the messy cleanup. In addition to having the ability to wag its tail Zoomer can understand English, Spanish, and French. In short when you buy/adopt a Zoomer it's like adding a member to the family.

At 4 feet 3 inches, one of the earlier models of the child-sized ASIMO is presently on display as an "attraction" at Disneyland—a place where a wish upon a star has been known to turn fantasy into reality. I would assert that making the first line of humanoid robots resemble children, at least in stature, is a stroke of genius. As is placing ASIMO is a place associated with the imagination and optimism of youth. Not to mention the fact that children who have normalized ASIMO in an amusement park will be more prone to accept a humanoid robot into their own homes as adults. To be clear, I am suggesting that Astro has already opened our doors to Zoomer and that ASIMO is still working on oiling the door hinges for Rosie.

Unlike Astro or Zoomer, Rosie poses a different kind of potential problem to the way we think about race and gender. More specifically, Rosie is designed to be read as a domestic servant or house slave. Rosie was for all intents and purposes is a mechanical mammy displaced from the Antebellum South and relocated to an animated futuristic utopia called America in 2062. In 1962 the television production company Hanna-Barbera (Willian Hanna and Joseph Barbera) speculates much further into the future than Yorkin ever imagines but what is frighteningly similar in their visions is humanity's dependency upon technologies of slavery.

The imagining of the character Rosie in the 1962 animated sitcom entitled *The Jetsons* raises several questions about the role humanoid robots might play in the household but also points to how race and gender might interact with technology to redefine the boundaries of human identity. Rosie was a domestic servant of the Jetson family. The Jetsons were written as the "average" white American middle-class family. The Jetsons included the father George Jetson (forty years old), mother Jane (thirty-three years old), and two children Judy (fifteen years old) and Elroy (six years old) and Astro the dog. George Jetson was employed as a well-paid button-pusher by a technology company called Spacely's Sprockets, and Jane was employed as the "home-keeper" despite the fact that the house slave Rosie maintain the household and managed the two

children. The Jetsons' household resembled the antebellum slave household in many respects. What is most striking about Rosie is her body.
Rosie was a morbidly obese pair-shaped humanoid robot. It was commonly stated in the narrative that Rosie was an outdated model but that
the Jetsons refused to trade her in for a newer model because of their
affections for her. Rosie did all the housework and most of the parenting
in addition to dispensing pills to the family for health and nutrition. In
many respects Rosie served the role as the classic mammy character. She
was characterized as being authoritarian and occasionally defiant. Although Rosie did not have a Southern accent, she was endowed with a
New Jersey accent despite the fact that the rest of the Jetsons spoke with a
non-distinct American dialect. In fact, only Rosie and Astro the Dog
(Astro was able to speak English with an impediment) spoke with devi-
ant dialects in the program. This in addition to her role as unpaid domestic servant and body shape located her is a space very similar to the
stereotypical mammy. The fact that Rosie also attempted to run away
from the Jetsons supports the comparison to Antebellum America. In
season 2 episode 2—"Rosie Come Home" of the *The Jetsons*, Rosie runs
away from home. Rosie tries to escape her employment with the Jetsons
because she feels that she is not appreciated. In truth, the problem is
Rosie's software has expired and is outdated. Rosie needs a new micro-
chip [*master*] cylinder. The performance of her duties has suffered and
irritated George Jetson to the point of verbally chastising Rosie despite
his earlier comment, "I never have to worry with Rosie around" (S2E2
"Rosie Come Home"). Feeling unwanted Rosie runs away from home to
find other employment but because of her age and model number, is
stuck doing menial labor worse than domestic service. On her quest to
find freedom/better employment she says, "Sure is tough for a robot in a
human's world" (S2E2). After visiting a used robot dealer[11] , at Robot
City, the Jetsons are persuaded to try a newer model of domestic robot.
Despite the fact that the dealer says, "Robot city has more parts than the
Milky Way has stars," (S2E2) he is fixed on selling them a new robot. He
even offers to accept Rosie as a trade-in for a newer model. Ultimately,
Rosie is unable to survive in human society alone and attempts to commit
suicide in a mechanized junkyard. At the last possible minute, George
Jetson and his family pull Rosie to safety. Upon returning to their home
Rosie is immediately upgraded with a new master cylinder and all is
back to business as usual. Rosie has proven herself to be a beloved member of the Jetson family but has also accepted her status as permanent
domestic servant with no hope or desire for freedom. Consequently, "Rosie Come Home" is the narrative of the contented machine unable to
transcend its domestic wiring.

In his book *Wired for War*, P. W. Singer asserts that the genre of science
fiction does not predict the future, but instead helps "readers rehearse for
the future" (Singer 159). Singer's book is largely about the employment of

robots in war. Beyond his discussion of drones and the practicality of using machines for killing as opposed to traditional soldiers, Singer's discussion is honest in its origin and destination of the robot concept. That is to say, the robot is probably headed exactly where we think it is, exactly where our imaginations will take it. Singer notes that science fiction has taken and is taking our imaginations to some familiar places that are invested in monetary gain, warfare, and servitude.

> It is often difficult to figure out just what the future will look like, but science fiction creates both an expectation and early acceptance of technologies that are not yet fully developed. As Bill Gates explains, *Star Trek* paved the way for his job at selling small, easy-to-use computers to the public. "It told the world that one day computers would be everywhere." He sees the same happening with robots from movies like *Star Wars* and *I, Robot*. "The popularity of robots in fiction indicates that people are receptive to the idea that these machines will one day walk among us as helpers and even companions." (Singer 164)

If Singer is correct in his assertion that such films and a plethora of other science fictive depictions of the future are "rehearsals for the future," trouble is on the way. The domestic robots found in films such as *Star Wars* and *I, Robot* share a frightening resemblance to antebellum slaves and eventually cause or at least participate in wars that take, instead of spare, many human lives. Already there is evidence that large-scale employment of robots will bring out the worst in humanity. "Robot Combat League: Rise of the Machine" premiered on February 26, 2013; on the Sci-Fi network. On Tuesday nights at 10 p.m. EST America can watch teams of everyday Americans use *exo-suits* to control fighting robots in a pit like gladiators of the past. It would appear that technology allows humanity to move toward the promise of the future while simultaneously holding onto the darkness of the past.

The slave community lied to itself about its true intents for the slave. Labor was never its sole function or intent. Contemporary society continues to tell itself the same lies about the advent of robotics. Cornel Lloyd loved the beautiful and voluptuous aunt Hester. He loved her and desired her as any man would love and desire a woman as beautiful and as human as him. Douglass' aunt Hester "was a woman of noble form, and of graceful proportions, having very few equals, and fewer superiors, in personal appearance, among the colored or white women of our neighborhood (Douglass 45). Aunt Hester was drop-dead gorgeous and as a result, Cornel Lloyd was at least infatuated with her to the point of forbidding her to have sexual relations with anyone but himself. Likewise, Harriet Jacob's Dr. Flint was madly in love with the young and beautiful Linda Brent. He loved her with a passion so great that it placed the fragile beauty of his own white and very human wife, Mrs. Flint, behind an elliptical shadow. Dr. Flint's love and desire was demonstrated by the erection of an edifice, not for a mere slave, but for a human woman that he imagined as a goddess. "When my master said he was going to build a house for me, and that he could do it with little trouble and expense, I was in hopes something would happen to frustrate his scheme; but I soon heard that the house was actually begun" (Jacobs 53). Humanity's quest to produce a machine in the image of a human is well on its way. Unfortunately, humanity's inability to be honest with itself about human nature promises to yield something very far removed from a utopia with friendly domestic servants. The placement of domestic humanoid robots in American households will undoubtedly influence definitions of gender and racial identity in very much the same way chattel slavery influenced the American identity.

## NOTES

1. The New ASIMO was first revealed in 2005, and represents significant advancements in robot mobility. ASIMO was created to be a helper to people. ASIMO's height of four feet, three inches (130 centimeters) makes it the perfect size for helping around the house, or assisting a person confined to a bed or a wheelchair. ASIMO's size also allows it to look directly at an adult sitting in a chair or sitting up in bed for easy and natural communication.

2. "Aristotle's theory of natural slavery, presented in Book I of the *Politics*, proved a godsend to pro-slavers in the Old South, as too those in other times and places wishing to promote or defend chattel slavery as an institution" (Millett 179).

3. Harlem Renaissance writer Nella Larsen is noted for her fiction engaging issues of racial identity and "passing" in her book entitled *Quicksand and Passing* [New Brunswick, New Jersey, Rutgers University Press, 1986].

4. Derrick Bell explores a similar scenario in his short story "The Space Traders," found in his book *Faces at the Bottom of the Well: The Permanence of Racism*, (New York: HarperCollins Publishers, 1992). Bell's speculative narrative considers what would happen if space travelers came to Earth and offered to take every African-American citizen away with them in exchange for thing like the cure for cancer, unlimited natural resources, and a cheap and clean energy source. The outcome of Bell's narrative is predicated on American history and does not bode well for the African-American.

5. The effort required in establishing American slavery as a legal institution was significant. In 1619 the first Africans were brought to Virginia as indentured servants, but it was not until the 1660's, almost forty years later, did the British Americas legalize slavery as an institution with laws known as slave codes.

6. The rule of race that I am referring to is borrowed from Toni Morrison's text *Playing in the Dark*. In her text Morrison asserts that in most American literature if the race of a character is not mentioned, it is imagined to be normative or white.

7. An extreme example of the intersection of technology and biology is addressed in the comedic novel *Machine Man* by Max Barry (New York: Vintage Books, 2011). After the scientist/engineer, Charles Neumann, loses his leg in an industrial accident he decides to build a new mechanical leg to replace the old. In the development of his new robotic leg, Neumann is overtaken by the idea of replacing his entire body with a stronger more durable and practical robotic body. Machine Man serves as a cautionary tale of what might happen when humans begin the process of miscegenation with robots.

8. Toni Morrison's *Playing in the Dark* asserts that in American Literature if race is not made evident in a novel the character of interest is white. I posit here that the same holds true in British literature as well.

9. To be clear, my statement is referring to humanoid domestic robots. There are in fact several models of small disc-like machines being sold in the American marketplace under the title of "robot." The iRobot Roomba 770, for example is a vacuum cleaner robot that is designed to clean the floors of its owners household automatically. Roomba vacuum robots range in price from 300–800 dollars and is usually available in one color, black. When asking the question of why Roomba, the companies answer is: Roomba cleans your floors like no vacuum has ever cleaned before—removing dirt, dust, pet hair and other debris all on its own. Using iAdapt® Responsive Navigation Technology, Roomba vacuums every section of your floor multiple times, getting under and around furniture and along wall edges, detecting dirt, avoiding stairs and navigating through loose wires to clean more of your room, more thoroughly.

10. Astro the Dog and Rosie the domestic robot were characters on an animated sitcom from 1962–63 produced by Hanna Barbera called *The Jetsons*.

11. The used robot dealer's job description is very similar to that of a slave trader.

## REFERENCES

Asimov, Isaac. *I, Robot*. (New York: Doubleday, 1950).

Calvert, Brian. "Slavery in Plato's Republic." *The Classical Quarterly*, Vol. 37, No. 2 (1987), pp. 367–372.

Capek, Karel. *R. U. R. (Rossum's Universal Robots)*. (London: Penguin Books, 2004).

Carby, Hazel. *Reconstructing Womanhood*. (New York: Oxford University Press, 1987).

Douglass, Frederick. *The Narrative of Life of Frederick Douglas*. (Boston: Bedford/St. Martin's. 2003).

Gong, Li. "The boundary of racial prejudice: Comparing preferences for computer-synthesized White, Black, and robot characters." *Computers in Human Behavior*; Sep. 2008, Vol. 24 Issue 5, p 2074–2093.

Hanna-Barbera. *Jetsons*, Season 2, Episode 2—"Come Home Rosie."

Hoppenstand, Gary. "Robots of the Past: Fitz-James O'Brien's "The Wondersmith." *Journal of Popular Culture*, Spring 1994, Vol 27, Issue 4, pages 13–30.

Jacobs, Harriet. *The Incidents in the Life of Girl*. (Cambridge: Harvard University Press, 1987).

Nakamura, Miri. "Marking bodily differences: mechanized bodies in Hirabayashi Hatsunosuke's 'Robot' and early Showa robot literature." *Japan Forum*, 19(2) 2007: p 169–190.

Millett, Paul. "Aristotle and Slavery in Athens." *Greece & Rome*, Second Series, Vol. 54, No. 2 (Oct., 2007), pp. 178–209

Odle, E.V. *The Clockwork Man*. (London: William Heinemann LFD, 1923).

Parrinder, Patrick. "Robots, Clones and Clockwork Men: The Post-Human Perplex in Early Twentieth-Century Literature and Science." *Interdisciplinary Science Reviews*, Vol. 34 No. 1, March, 2009, 56–67.

Reid Simmons, Maxim Makatchev, Rachel Kirby, Min Kyung Lee, Imran Fanaswala, Brett Browning, Jodi Forlizzi, Majd Sakr, "Believable

Richardson, Kathleen. "Mechanical People." *New Scientist*; 6/24/2006, Vol. 190 Issue 2557, p. 56–57.

Robertson, Jennifer. "Gendering Humanoid Robots: Robo-Sexism in Japan." *Body and Society*; Jun. 2010, Vol. 16 Issue 2, p. 1–36.

Rousseau, Jean-Jacques. *On the Social Contract, Discourse on the Origin of Inequality, Discourse on Political Economy*. Translated and Edited by Donald A. Cress. (Indianapolis, Indiana: Hackett Publishing Company, 1983).

Robot Characters." *Association for the Advancement of Artificial Intelligence* WINTER 2011, pages 39–52.

Yorkin, Nicole. "A Day in the Life: A Family of Four and Their Robots, 25 Years From Now." *Los Angeles Times Magazine*, April 3, 1988. Pgs. 8–23.

# TWO

# Proslavery Thought and the Black Robot

## Selling Household Appliances to Southern Belles

This chapter is a critical examination of the rhetoric that is used in framing the inevitable integration of humanoid robotic technology into the common American household. This chapter will compare the rhetoric used in antebellum proslavery literature to rhetoric used in contemporary speculative fiction and popular culture with the intent to show how all too often history and physical fact are trumped by rhetoric and good advertisement. Texts that will be engaged are to include the play "The Benevolent Planter" by Thomas Bellamy; the science fiction short story "Robbie" by Asimov; *Wired for War* by P. W. Singer and various essays from *The Ideology of Slavery: Proslavery Thought in the Antebellum South, 1830–1860,* and *Proslavery: A History of the Defense of Slavery in America, 1701–1840,* edited by Faust and Tise, respectively. By examining the antebellum texts mentioned, I hope to show how the analogy of chattel slavery and social progress might be equated to contemporary technological advances in robotics and the imagining of a social utopia. The importance of pursuing such a line of thought is to consider the dangers that might evolve in a society that chooses to become dependent on any notion of slavery, even if it involves the enslavement of technology such as automobiles, televisions, cell phones, the Internet, and perhaps humanoid robots with AI.

Rhetoric is by definition a tool of persuasion, which is dependent upon the employment of Aristotelian devices known as logos, pathos, and ethos. It is an art form that has been employed to manipulate the opinion of individuals and groups targeting emotion, social ethics, and logic. Rhetoric is and always has been a device designed to police thought with regards to specific topics and or issues that are not agreed upon by all. Rhetoric has been an invaluable tool in shaping both modern and ancient societies with regards to law and morality. Thus, it only stands to reason that rhetoric would play a crucial role in the process of defining and valuing property in society. If used effectively rhetoric can be a salesman's greatest tool. One only has to switch on a television or computer to see the power of rhetoric in the great western market place. There is quite literally nothing that the deployment of effective rhetoric cannot sell to the willing American consumer. If an American doesn't want to buy it, it's only because they have not been exposed to the appropriate commercial (rhetorical device) yet.

In the case of American slavery, rhetoric was used to both combat as well as justify the dehumanization and subjugation of black bodies. Rhetoric was adroitly employed to facilitate the process of imagining abducted Africans as objects and possessions without human rights, subject to the desires of their masters. "But given the nature of exploitation, the assimilation of a human being to an object, or even to and animal, is an untenable and contradictory fiction" (Meillassoux 9). To be clear, if slaves were truly and consistently imagined as objects and soulless chattel, slavery would present no advantages over the use of simple machines and beasts of burden. The humanity of the slave was both required, and denied, in order to justify the institutionalization of slavery. Such an obvious contradiction seemed to depend upon the implementation of the appropriate balance of rhetoric and economic motivation in order to succeed, even if only for a relatively brief period in American history.

In her text *Fanatical Schemes: Proslavery Rhetoric and the Tragedy of Consensus*, Patricia Roberts-Miller convincingly argues that American slavery was not only an economic and political institution—slavery was a "rhetorical construct" (Roberts-Miller 18). Roberts-Miller asserts that because people argued for and against slavery as an institution, the process of debate implicitly and explicitly defined the institution. With this suggestion, Roberts-Miller positions the discussion of slavery beyond a simply physical atrocity of black bodies during a particular period in American history and places it into a metaphysical realm that allows for a closer analysis of how the institution of slavery might manifest itself into the imagination of a society. Without negating any of the importance of the physical slaves themselves, I would like to employ Robert-Miller's assertions about how rhetoric shaped the institution of slavery in the minds of American consumers with the hope that such an investigation might shed light onto how a similar "rhetorical construct" in contemporary society might yield similar debates and very similar results with regard to human/robotic identity and social order.

Drew Gilpin Faust in his *The Ideology of Slavery: Proslavery Thought in the Antebellum South, 1830–1860*, notes that slavery was the medium for the discussion of several "fundamental social issues such as the meaning of natural law, the desire for freedom and order, the relationship between tradition and progress, as well as equality, dependence, and autonomy" (Faust 2). Faust's collection of essays supports the notion that although slavery was always morally suspect it was defended by large numbers of southerners and northerners as well as "Britons in England and the West Indies throughout the eighteenth and early nineteenth centuries" through the time of the Civil War (Faust 3). In many respects slavery was the topic upon which American identity was constructed both literally and metaphorically. With the help of political rhetoric and propaganda slavery helped produce the American mythology of a southern way of life, "it served for Americans generally as a means of reassessing the profoundest assumptions on which their world was built" (Faust 4). The idea of slavery, not necessarily its physical and historical reality, became the lie that antebellum Americans believed to be a requirement for their evolution as a nation.

Contrary to common belief, the idea that chattel slavery was understood as being morally indefensible was widely accepted in both northern and southern regions of America in as early as the eighteenth century. By the nineteenth century, debate about the economic and moral volatility of the institution of slavery was commonplace in the north and south. In many regards, rhetoric and the politics that generated it hid the fact that southerners and slave owners questioned the morality of slavery. Many southerners viewed slavery as a sort of "necessary evil" necessary for the erection of a Republic. Robert Walsh notes:

> We do not deny, in America, that great abuses and evils accompany our negro slavery. The plurality of the leading men of the southern states, are so well aware of its pestilent genius, that they would glad see it abolished, if this were feasible with benefit to the slaves, and without inflicting on the country, injury of such a magnitude as no community has ever voluntarily incurred. (Walsh 421)

As Walsh implicitly asserts, slave owners were aware that slavery was "bad," but apparently, there were greater things at stake, other than the freedom and humanity of a fellow human being, albeit of a darker complexion and foreign origin. Walsh suggests that the livelihood of a nation was at stake, and that without the slave there could be no American community. The phrase "pestilent genius" is a frighteningly accurate way of describing how the institution of slavery was imagined in America pre-Civil War as it acknowledges slavery's ability to destroy the moral and social order of a society while so creatively providing the workforce and scapegoats necessary to stabilize a national economy and identity. Walsh would have his audience believe that the slave was essential for the development of a Republic, as referenced by Plato. Slavery then, was an unpleasant tool required for the building of a healthy economy and national community. As stated in chapter one of this book, slavery was perceived by many to be a sort of technological tool required for social advancement and evolution. The historian Larry E. Tise presents an even clearer perspective of the discussion of slavery in his text entitled *Proslavery: A History of the Defense of Slavery in America, 1701–1840*, where he asserts that "proslavery ideology was a mode of thinking, a concatenation of ideas, and a system of symbols that expressed the social, cultural, and moral values of a large portion of the population of America in the first half of the nineteenth century" (Tise xv). It is my intent to convincingly argue that the mode of thinking that Tise references is a product of the rhetoric that was being employed at the time and is indicative of the rhetoric being employed presently to facilitate a new slavery dependent upon technological advances in the fields of robotics and artificial intelligence.

*What Art Tells Us*

*The Benevolent Planters* is a play by Thomas Bellamy that was used as a proslavery propaganda tool by anti-abolitionists in the nineteenth century. Proslavery advocates also sought the support of the creative community including artists, poets and writers. In fact Bellamy's play was written in response to an antislavery poem entitled "The Negro's Complaint," by William Cowper, a poet invested in the abolition of slavery and the author of several overtly antislavery poems, although not as popular as the 1788 publication of "The Negro's Complaint." Cowper's poem was a scathing rebuke to the notion that slavery was anything other than a cruel and inhuman institution developed to line the pockets of British tyrants with gold.

In "The Negro's Complaint," Cowper gives voice to Africans "forced from home and all its pleasures to increase a stranger's treasurers" (line 3). In short, Cowper's poem acts as an effective piece of rhetoric targeting the pathos and ethos of its readers suggesting hope for the slave via the potentially unbounded nature of imagination and the mind. "Minds are never to be sold" (line 8). Cowper suggests that there are elements of a conscious slave that cannot be enslaved. The mind and the imagination that it manifests is unbounded and impossible to permanently fetter.

Bellamy's drama tells the story of two black lovers, Oran and Selima, who are separated in Africa and end up living on adjoining plantations in the West Indies. The story suggests their idle and easy life in Africa is replaced by a god-fearing, productive and structured life of toil on a plantation. In many respects Bellamy's drama is an excellent example of the mythology of the "white man's burden." That is to say, the act of "relocating" black Africans from African to the Americas was an act of Christian charity, not intended to be associated with acts of inhumanity or genocide. Bringing slaves to the new world was a Christian responsibility invested in exposing as many pagan and benighted souls to the righteous light of Jesus Christ.[1] It also suggests that the two planters "Goodwin" and "Heartfee" are decent individuals who have a paternal interest in the well being of their slaves. To be sure, the paternal interests of slave owners of the past are too easily translated and blurred with proprietary feelings and behaviors that accompany objects (household appliances or pets) as opposed to subjects.

Isaac Asimov's short story "Robbie" is an excellent example of how the past is inextricable from the future. Asimov's speculative narrative of a little girl and her robotic nanny yields frighten similarity to Antebellum America, but more importantly it demonstrates how rhetoric is used to sell the notion of slavery as an acceptable and useful commodity despite its moral instability. Robbie is a humanoid robot from head to toe. Although his body is similar to that of a human, his metallic skin and "metal feet" mark Robbie as a nonhuman machine (Asimov 1). However, it is not simply the exterior appearance of Robbie that defines his character beyond that of a walking appliance. We are introduced to Robbie along side his charge and companion, Gloria Weston, an eight-year-old flesh and blood child very invested in her emotionally charged playtime with Robbie.

As Robbie and Gloria play a game of hide-and-seek it is made clear that Robbie is in possession of a consciousness and emotion at least as complex as the little girl's with which he is engaged. It is at this juncture in the narrative that Asimov's short story becomes a critical analysis of the relationship of master and slave far beyond a science fictive fairytale. It is Robbie's ability to feel, whether artificial or organic, that places him in the category of *him* instead of *it*. Robbie's artificial intelligence (AI) along with his performance of "humanity" elevates his status from a simple machine to a sentient being. Robbie is a being made in the likeness of a human. He is a being given human characteristics and abilities by his human creators. Although Robbie is not completely or biologically human, he is undeniably a product of humanity and is thus part human. Robbie's silver metal skin "kept at a constant temperature of seventy by high resistant coils" locates his body in the realm of human possibility. Like the slaves of Antebellum America with their brown skin and aesthetic difference, Robbie is at least imagined as human in the minds of his creators and employers.

Gloria's presence in the narrative is the medium by which the rhetorical devices pathos and ethos are employed to demonstrate Robbie's soul. Through Robbie's interaction with Gloria, the reader is made aware of Robbie's ability to love and care for another human beyond basic programming. For example, "Robbie was hurt at the unjust accusation" of peeking during a game of hide-and-seek (Asimov 4). Furthermore, "hardhearted Robbie paid scant attention" (Asimov 4) to Gloria's threat to cry, when he initially does not allow her to ride on his shoulders.

Robbie is written as more than a soulless machine programed to protect a little girl. On the contrary, Robbie loves little Gloria with conscious thought and intelligence. Without this ability it is unlikely that Mr. and Mrs. Weston would entrust their child with Robbie. As stated earlier, the humanity of the slave is both required and denied by the master.

Like the Bellmont household, mentioned in Harriet Wilson's novel *Our Nig: Sketches from the Life of a Free Black, in a Two-Story White House, North. Showing That Slavery's Shadow Fall Even There* (1959), the Weston household is also divided by the issue of robotics/slavery. Where Frado, the biracial (white mother, black/African father) protagonist of *Our Nig* is haunted by the presence of Mrs. Bellmont, Robbie is also very weary of Mrs. Weston. "Gloria's mother was always a source of uneasiness to Robbie and there was always the impulse to sneak away from her sight" (Asimov 6). Gloria's father on the other hand "was rarely home in the daytime except on Sunday" and when he was present in the household "he proved a genial and understanding person" (Asimov 6). Both the Weston and Bellmont households seem divided to various degrees by the issue of the domestic servant. According to Hazel Carby's *Reconstructing Womanhood*, the Belmont home might be read as a symbol of a nation divided by regions, north and south—a country experiencing a civil war. I would only go as for as to say that the Weston's seem to be experiencing a domestic disagreement. Unlike the civil war in the Bellmont household the removal of the domestic servant does not resolve the disturbance in the Weston home. In fact, for the Westons, Robbie's presence seems to be required in order to resolve the domestic disturbance that his identity has facilitated.

If Mrs. Bellmont can be read as a Southern Belle, Mr. Bellmont might be read as a sympathetic white northerner. "Mrs. Bellmont, the white mistress, was described as having power over the whole family—husband, sons, daughters, and Frado—and was symbolic of the power of the South" (Carby 46). As such, Mr. Belmont is written as ineffectual and hesitant to fully invest in the protection and freedom of Frado. A similar method of reading might be applied to Mr. Weston. Although he is in favor of Robbie's presence in his home and companionship with his daughter Gloria, he is ultimately submissive to his wife, Grace Weston.

> And yet he loved his wife—and what was worse, his wife knew it. George Weston, after all was only a man—poor thing—and his wife made full use of every device, which a clumsier and more scrupulous sex has learned, with reason and futility, to fear. (Carby 11)

The above passage is insightful because it speaks directly to the devises of antislavery rhetoric that Mrs. Weston, a representative of abolition, used to persuade her husband, the representative of proslavery, to get Robbie out of their home. Conversely, the roles of Mr. and Mrs. Bellmont experience a similar dilemma with varying results. Both Mrs. Bellmont and Weston appeal to their husband' ethos, pathos, and logos. Mrs. Weston notes that their village has grown to fear Robbie because of his difference and that safety of their child might be in jeopardy. She makes the suggestion that the community they live in will harshly judge their family and that if he does not conform to the general consensus about robots, life will become unbearable. She notes the newly established laws pertaining to robot curfews and the fact that the employment of Robbie as a domestic servant is an issue that spans further than the privacy of his household. Likewise, Mr. Bellmont and his son would rather leave the two-story house than accept the "tyrannical rages" of Mrs. Bellmont (Carby 44). Unfortunately, both men only offer sympathy and loud protest for the treatment of Frado. Both men are hesitant to jeopardize the two-story-house, which was an allegory for the seemingly divided nation. Seeming, because Wilson's narrative acts as evidence that the nation was not so distinctly divided on the issues of slavery, as some versions of history would suggest. David Dowling's article, "Other and More Terrible Evils: Anti-capitalist Rhetoric In Harriet Wilson's *Our Nig* and Proslavery Propaganda," provides a reading of Wilson's narrative that suggests the employment of rhetoric was more pervasive than the actual issues of slavery and that regional difference was a rhetorically constructed mythology. Frado's experience both reveals the hypocrisy of the North in regard to the forced labor and abuse of slaves as well as its desire and intent to manipulate and capitalize on a marginalized labor force. Dowling notes that, "proslavery propaganda exposing unfair labor conditions suffered by northern blacks was all but unheard of before the Civil War" (Dowling 131). Thus Wilson's narrative provided insight into much more complex and united national identity than a divided nation would suggest.

When Grace does finally cajole George to have Robbie sent back to the "factory" Gloria becomes ill. The dog that Grace replaces Robbie with is found to be an unsatisfactory companion for Gloria. Ultimately, George develops a plan to reunite his daughter and Robbie in New York. For the Belmont family the civil war ends with the removal of Frado from their household. The abolition of slavery, or in the case of Frado, indentured servitude, results in the two-story house or the United States reuniting. All too simply stated, *Our Nig* demonstrates the ill effects of the institution of slavery, but also the mythology of regional difference regarding to the ideology of slavery. Wilson's text clearly asserts that slavery was nation wide and that imaginary boundaries of free and slave states had little or no effect on the imagination of the American populous during Antebellum America. Americans wanted America to prosper and slavery was a means to that end. If Grace represents the wellbeing of the American economy, it is clear that without the advancement and full employment of technology the wellbeing of the American economy of today and tomorrow would be cast into jeopardy.

*The Idea of the Slave/Robot:*

In *The Problem of Slavery: In the Age of Emancipation*, David Davis explains, among other things related to slavery in American history, how the idea of slavery took hold in America and how it used "animalization[2] "and philosophy as justification for its institutionalization. In the North, beginning during the Revolution and continuing through the first decade of the next century, state by state emancipation legislation was passed, although in the larger slaveholding states such as Virginia and South Carolina abolition was phased out over several decades. By 1810, 75 percent of Northern slaves had been freed and virtually all were freed within the next generation. During this period the utility of the slave in Northern states had decreased significantly. In the United States, the antislavery contention that slavery was both economically inefficient and socially detrimental to the country as a whole were more prevalent than philosophical and moral arguments against slavery. In Virginia, as the economy shifted away from tobacco towards less labor-intensive wheat crops, more slaves were freed between 1783 and 1812 than any time until 1865. There was the potential, in many Southern minds, for a relatively short transition away from slavery. However, this perspective rapidly changed as the worldwide demand for sugar and cotton from America increased and the Louisiana Purchase opened up vast new territories ideally suited for a plantation economy. The point that I would like to make here is that slavery only becomes a national issue of contention when the demand for slave labor increases. And to be clear, it is only a point of contention politically. The common American from the north or south simply views the shift in the economy as an opportunity to build wealth. Roberts-Miller notes that were it not for abolitionist rhetoric, the institution of slavery and possibly the slaves themselves might have never moved beyond the mundane.[3] A slave was a tool used to make money. As such, in the imaginations of most landowning Americans living in the north or south, a slave was an appliance required for the production of goods and the procurement of wealth.

Only in the early nineteenth century did abolitionist movements gather momentum, and many countries abolished slavery in the first half of the 19th century. The increasing rarity of slavery, combined with an increase in the number of slaves caused by a boom in the cotton trade, drew attention and criticism to the Southern states' continuation of slavery. Faced with this growing "antislavery" movement, slaveholders and their sympathizers began to articulate an explicit defense of slavery. To be clear, it must be understood that slaveholders did not only reside in Southern states. There were many businessmen who owned and invested in plantations whose profit very much depended on slavery.

The *Mudsill Speech* (1858) by James Henry Hammond and John C. Calhoun's *Speech in the US Senate* (1837) articulated the pro-slavery political argument during the period at which the ideology was at its most mature (late 1830s–early 1860s). These pro-slavery theorists championed a class-sensitive view of American antebellum society. They felt that the bane of many past societies was the existence of the class of the landless poor. Pro-slavery theorists felt that this class of landless poor was inherently transient and easily manipulated, and as such prone to destabilized society as a whole. Thus, the greatest threat to democracy was seen as coming from class warfare that destabilized a nation's economy, society, government, and threatened the peaceful and harmonious implementation of laws.

This theory supposes that there must be, and supposedly always has been, a lower class for the upper classes to rest upon. This theory was used by its composer Senator and Governor James Henry Hammond, a wealthy plantation owner, to justify what he saw as the willingness of the non-whites to perform menial work that enabled the higher classes to move civilization forward. With this in mind, any efforts for class or racial equality that ran counter to the theory would inevitably run counter to civilization itself. This line of thinking closely resembles the thought behind the construction of utopian societies. David Davis notes that Aristotle contemplated the social stratifications of his time and concluded that, "some men are marked out for subjection, and others for rule" (Davis 35). According to Aristotle, slaves and women were designed by nature to have stronger bodies and weaker minds than free people [white men]. Much like the biological robots found in Karel Capek's 1921 drama *R. U. R.*, the slave is inhuman (despite its human likeness), and should not be mistaken for human if the utopian society is to come to fruition. Domin is careful to explain this to Helena:

> My dear Miss Glory, Robots are not people. They are mechanically more perfect than we are, they have an astounding intellectual capacity, but they have no soul. Oh, Miss Glory, the creation of an engineer is technically more refined than the product of nature (Capek 9).

It is as if Capek was responding to Aristotle's theory of social order in the above passage as he suggests that the notion of slavery is justifiable through nature and technology.[4]

Pro-slavery theorists asserted that slavery eliminated this problem by elevating all free people to the status of "citizen," and removing the landless poor from the political process entirely by means of enslavement. Thus, those who would most threaten economic stability and political harmony were not allowed to undermine a democratic society, because they were not allowed to participate in it. So, in the mindset of pro-slavery men, slavery was for protecting the common good of slaves, masters, and society as a whole. Slavery was the means by which a utopian society could be brought about. I assert that the same quest for an economic utopia will become manifest with the advent of humanoid robots.

That is to say that if household and office appliances can play the role of the landless poor or the lower classes, humans, at least in theory, should be elevated to a social status that will look better than what they experienced before the enslavement of the robot.

Such speculation has already entered the imagination of American capitalist thinkers as demonstrated in Chris Farrell's 2010 article "Will Robots Create Economic Utopia." Farrell noted that,

> [I]t's easy to imagine a dystopian future defined by technological unemployment and underemployment for the mass of workers. Yet the rise of an automated, digitized economy is wonderful news. The potential efficiency gains and productivity improvements are mind-boggling. We're at an inflection point comparable to the First Industrial Revolution in the 18th century and the Second Industrial Revolution a century later (Farrell).

Farrell's article is primarily concerned with the distribution of wealth generated from such a robotic driven economy and the presence of job security for humans. There is no mention of terms like slavery or morality. Robot working conditions or robotic healthcare plans have not made their way into the imaginations of economists and businessmen because the nations' economic future does not factor in questions of AI and the problems that it will undoubtedly create. The mind-boggling productive improvements that might occur because of the employment of a robotic labor force will not allow large corporations to consider the level of AI that will be required and its influence on the identity and consciousness of the machines employed. It is the inflection point that Farrell notes that will unfortunately disallow the business minded world from considering how technological advancements my effect definitions of humanity. Just as monetary gain and economic stability were the driving forces behind American chattel slavery and processes of dehumanization yesterday, the technological advancements in the fields of robotics and AI will also pose considerable threats to how humanity is imagined tomorrow. Chattel slavery had irrevocable effects on identity construction in America and the world. It has influenced how societies are shaped and will continue to be shaped for centuries to come. Quite frankly, American chattel slavery has left a legacy that cannot be escaped. As a byproduct of slavery, racism is a system of advantage based on race that continues to impede the very national identity it was constructed to serve.[5] Whether the slave is of flesh and blood or metal, slavery will negatively affect both the master and the slave.[6] For despite the profit that slavery may yield, it has historically and irrefutably caused social and psychological injury to an entire nation. To repeat such a monumentally tragic error in human history on the rhetoric that technology will not intersect with humanity and morality is nothing short of criminal. The rate at which technology is being disseminated into the American public along with the rhetoric that promotes continued social dependency on newer technologies should confirm any doubts that the past *could* repeat itself.

## NOTES

1. See "On Being Brought from Africa to America" by Phillis Wheatley.

2. David Davis employs the terms animalization or dehumanization synonymously. Animalization is the "treatment of slaves as if they were domesticated animals." It refers to the impossibility of converting humans into totally compliant, submissive, accepting chattels symbolized by Aristotle's ideal of the "natural slave" (Preface xiii).

3. In "For the sake of your wives and children and their posterity: Manly Politics," Roberts-Miller suggests that the contention of slavery was not about slavery itself, but how various political parties chose to speak or not speak about the issue of slavery and the social and economic threat that it presented. "It was about which political party could respond in the most manly way to the 'threat' supposedly presented by their criticism of slavery"(126).

4. Capek's drama entitled *Rossum's Universal Robot* makes the suggestion that the robot is not regional or specific to a particular group or nationality. Rossum's robots/slaves are to be utilized universally regardless of global location.

5. This definition of racism is borrowed from Beverly Tatum and her 2003 publication entitled *Why Are All the Black Kids Sitting Together in the Cafeteria: And Other Conversations About Race.*

6. In Frederick Douglass' 1845 slave narrative he notes that "slavery proved as injurious to her as it did to me," (66) in reference to Mrs. Auld and her fall into the institution of slavery.

## REFERENCES

Asimov, Isaac. *I, Robot*. New York: Bantam Dell, 1950.

Capek, Karel. *R. U. R. (Rossum's Universal Robots)*. London: Penguin Books, 2004.

Carby, Hazel. *Reconstructing Womanhood: The Emergence of the Afro-American Woman Novelist*. New York: Oxford University Press, 1987.

Cowper, William. "The Negro's Complaint," http://www.yale.edu/glc/aces/cowper2.htm.

Davis, Davis Brion. *The Problem of Slavery in the Age of Emancipation*. New York: Alfred A. Knopf, 2014.

Douglass, Frederick. *Narrative of the Life of Frederick Douglass An American Slave Written by Himself*. Boston/New York: Bedford/ St. Martin's Press, 2003.

Dowling, David. "Other and More Terrible Evils": Anticapitalist Rhetoric in Harriet Wilson's *Our Nig* and Proslavery Propaganda." *College Literature* 36.3 [Summer 2009]. Pgs. 116–136.

Farrell, Chris. "Will Robots Create Economic Utopia." www.businessweek.com/articles/2013–02–11/will-robots-create-economic-utopia.

Faust, Drew Gilpin. Editor of *The Ideology of Slavery: Proslavery Thought in the Antebellum South, 1830–1860*. Louisiana: Louisiana State University Press, 1981.

Meillassoux, Claude. *The Anthropology of Slavery: The Womb of Iron and Gold*. London and Chicago: Athlone and University of Chicago Press, 1991.

Tise, Larry E. *Proslavery: A History of the Defense of Slavery in America, 1701–1840*. Athens, Georgia: University of Georgia Press, 1987.

Walsh, Robert. *An Appeal from the Judgments of Great Britain*. Mitchell, Ames, and White; William Brown, printer, 1819. New York: Negro Universities Press, 1969.

# THREE

## The True Cult of Humanhood

*Displacing Repressed Sexuality onto Mechanical Bodies*

This chapter examines the employment of racial and gender stereotypes in the construction of robots in the American imagination. It attempts to explains how images of the Sapphire, Jezebel, and Mammy are distorted into the gynoid—a sexualized mechanical body. Hazel Carby's *Reconstructing Womanhood* is used to speculate on the role of female robots and the results of displacing sexual repressed desires onto machines instead of humans. This chapter seeks to understand why robots and slaves will always be better lovers than their creators. And ultimately, this chapter is concerned with the parameters of humanity, which will undoubtedly be highlighted with the employment of humanoid machines.

David Levy's book *Love and Sex with Robots: The Evolution of Human-Robot Relationships* is startling not because it convincingly speculates the mental and physical relationships that will evolve between humans and machines in the near future, but because of his very careful explanation of how such relationships will evolve. Levy's narrative sounds almost identical to how slaves were imagined in Antebellum America and how African-Americans were eventually accepted as American citizens worthy of all human and civil rights that were denied their progenitors less than 50 years ago.[1] Levy's detailed explanation of how "robots will transform human notions of love and sexuality" provides a lens that is remarkably similar to the perspective used to understand how the African-American (previously referred to as the American slave) has been transformed in the American imagination. Levy speaks of the robot and technological advances that are both realities and in various states of development. His adroit understanding of the possibilities of human technology accentuates his keen understanding of the human psyche and

29

its evolution. Levy's book asserts that despite the seemingly fantastic elements surrounding humanoid robots, humanity will acclimate to an unavoidable future. Remarkably, Levy's meditation on the future seems rooted in the past in a fashion that facilitates a critical understanding of how the slave was imagined by the master class as well as how the African-American identity has been formulated and imagined in America. Levy's text convincingly argues that robots will move into a space in the human imagination that is very analogous to the role played by the African-America slave. Furthermore, Levy's conclusions about he the future suggest that the robot will inevitably be imagined as far more than a machine in the hearts and minds of a many humans.

John Blassingame's seminal 1972 text, *The Slave Community: Plantation Life in the Antebellum South,* established the origin and psychology behind several stereotypes used in the imagining of marginalized black bodies. More specifically, the Nat (Turner), Sambo, and Jack stereotypes are discussed to explain the complexity and contradictory components of the slave personalities. "Nat was the incorrigible runaway, the poisoner of white men, the ravager of white women who defied the rules of plantation society." (Blassingame 225). Sambo was a hybrid stereotype including the loyal Uncle Tom, the faithful Uncle Remus, and the dishonest Jim Crow. Unfortunately, Blassingame's insightful observations fail to shed light on the development of female personalities employed by the plantation slave culture.

> While acknowledging that an analysis of one male slave stereotype will not allow access to an understanding of mythology of the "Old South," Blassingame accepted that a dissection of the complex of male stereotypes could provide this understanding. The relationship between male and female representations and the complex and contradictory nature of figurations of the black woman as slave was ignored. (Carby 21)

The Mammy, Sapphire, and the Jezebel are three very important images of female slaves that seem to figure into the way black women and the female robot will and are imagined even in the twenty-first century. The Mammy archetype suggested an asexual female domestic servant intent in the duties of child rearing and managing the domicile for the mistress of the household. Physically the Mammy was imagined as being dark of complexion and morbidly obese yet having possession of great physical strength. The Mammy was easily identifiable as a guardian of the masters' household and children. As mentioned in chapter one of this meditation, the robot in Asimov's short story "Robbie" very closely follows the example of the Mammy archetype. The Jezebel in many respects was the antithesis of the Victorian white woman described and bounded by the four cardinal virtues of womanhood within the Cult of True Womanhood. The Jezebel was sexuality personified—a sexually promiscuous black woman with an insatiable sexual appetite endowed with unbounded levels of fertility. The Jezebel was deemed absent of modesty and prone to enjoy sensual dancing, immoral thinking and was possessed of masculine persona as a result of her oversexed nature. The Sapphire also rejected the laws of white feminine virtue. Furthermore, the Sapphire like the Mammy was possessed of herculean strength, which was used to emasculate male slaves and to terrorize slave children. Where the Mammy at least demonstrated the feminine ability to nurture children, the Sapphire lacked any maternal abilities associated with traditional western motherhood. In *Reconstructing Womanhood*, Hazel Carby is accurate when she notes that, "the black female was excluded from the parameters of virtuous possibilities" (Carby 27). To be clear, the archetypes and the actual female slaves being referred to in the antebellum period were not initially imagined as human "women." They were chattel or more appropriately, biological machines with crude gender assignments. I would posit that black "women" and robots, especially those being designed for the sex industry mentioned by Levy are one in the same in the imaginations of their designers despite the obvious differences in biological and technological origins. I would go even further by asserting that this blurring between human and machine in our imaginations has been facilitated by literature, film, and popular culture.

The characters Pris and Rachael Rosen from Philip K. Dick's classic science fiction novel, *Do Androids Dream of Electric Sheep (1968)*, serve as excellent examples of how Levy's predictions about humanity's relationship with robotic technology might develop and begin to blur identity boundaries. Pris is a pleasure model and Rachael is a "sales device for prospective emigrants" (Dick 60). The protagonist of the Dick's narrative is Decker, a human police officer/detective assigned the task of deactivating a group of renegade androids. Decker imagines the androids in very much the same way an overseer or slave owner might image an attractive female slave in Antebellum America.

> Some female androids seemed to him pretty; he had found himself physically attracted by several, and it was an odd sensation, knowing intellectually that they were machines, but emotionally reacting anyway (Decker 95).

In 1982 Ridley Scott directed *Blade Runner*, a modified film adaptation of Dick's *Do Androids Dream of Electric Sheep* novel. The film like the book depicts a twenty-first century dystopian Los Angeles where robots have been integrated into mainstream society. The humanoid robot or "Replicant" has been developed to a point where they have become indistinguishable from "normal" human beings. "The Nexus 6 Replicants were superior in strength and agility, and at least equal in intelligence, to the genetic engineers who created them" (*Blade Runner*). The Replicants were used as slave labor in the hazardous exploration and colonization of other planets. Their jobs were varying in nature and included positions in the military (combat models/assassins), and entertainment (standard pleasure models or sex robots). Leon (trickster), Roy Batty (leader), Zhora (beauty and the beast), and Pris are the four replicants that Decker is assigned to "retire" for the Tyrell Corporation. All Nexus 6 are designed to copy human beings in every way including the development of human emotion. As a result each Nexus 6 is programmed with a fail-safe four-year life span. The shortened life span of the four replicants motivates them to seek out their creator (Eldon Tyrell) in order to procure a longer duration of life.

Rachael is a Nexus 6 owned by the Tyrell Corporation who will serve as the test subject for Deckard's replicant detection device, the Voight-Kampff machine. It is both interesting and important to note that the same archetypes used to imagine slaves in antebellum America are also employed to imagine the robots of the future. Rachael is clearly written as the tragic mulatto. Her moment of awakening or realization occurs when Deckard tells her that her memories are all implants taken from the experiences of Eldon Tyrell's human niece, and not her own. The scene is very reminiscent of Frances E. W. Harper's character Iola Leroy[2] when she is informed that she is not what she has been led to believe all of her life. Where Iola learns that she is black, Rachael must accept the fact that she is an android created by the Tyrell Corporation.[3]

The slave archetypes seem to fit effortlessly onto the characters of the biological machines in the film *Blade Runner*. Roy Batty is the Nat Turner who is intelligent and very willing to employ violence as a tool to gain his freedom, which for the android seems to be equivalent to more time to live his life. Leon is also intelligent but takes on the guise of an unintelligent worker in order to infiltrate the Tyrell Corporation as a manual laborer. Leon plays the role of the Sambo or Step-and-Fetch-it archetype—allowing the master to believe that the slave is harmless and unable to complete physically and or mentally challenging tasks, all the while deceiving the master and awaiting an opportunity to kill the master and his family for the sake of freedom. Zorah fits the role of Sapphire with her physical prowess and employment of violence. Pris is by definition a Jezebel—a manipulator of men via her sexual attributes and proclivity to be dishonest and immoral.

In both film and novel Deckard is written as the slave catcher of the future. He hunts down the most dangerous kinds of slaves known to mankind—the slave that can pass for human. Deckard hunts replicants (copies of humans who have greater intellect, greater physical strength, and more humanity than humans have themselves). The slaves that Deckard hunts in *Blade Runner* only seek to extend their abbreviated lives. They have no desire to destroy humanity or disrupt the already post-apocalyptic sparsely populated Earth. It is their ability to pass as human that makes them a threat to Deckard and his employers. The existence of robots that might redefine or blur the definition of humanity is more of a threat than violent robots. Consequently, mythologies of murderous robots like the mythologies of violent and oversexed slaves are put in the imaginations of the populous to stabilize that which has never been stable, humanity. Zorah, played by Joanna Cassidy, is posing as an exotic dancer when Deckard finds her changing room backstage after performing at a seedy burlesques dive. He watches her strip and shower off her serpent costume, which symbolizes her characters relationship to biblical images of evil and temptation, but also speaks to Deckard's questionable morality and desire for Zorah's unlawful body. Zorah is portrayed as both sexy and dangerous as she handily beats Deckard like a rag doll after she sees through his poorly performed disguise as an agent of the "Confidential Committee on Moral Abuses." Just as she is about to strangle him to death she is interrupted by a troop of actors returning to the changing room after a performance. The painted faces and costumes that are worn by the actors including Zorah, suggest a minstrel show where androids and humans wear a sort of blackface to entertain the populous. The interruption of witnesses inexplicably causes to Zorah to flee the scene before she is able to kill Deckard. As Deckard chases Zorah through the crowded urban streets that take on the semblance of a forest or heavily populated jungle of lights and glass, the comparison of Zorah and a runaway slave becomes evident. Deckard shoots through a crowd of bystanders as if to imply that the death of a "replicant" was more important than the death of a human stuck on Earth and too dumb to move out of the way of his explosive bullets, to the safety of an off-planet colony. The assassination of Zorah is one of the more memorable scenes in the *Blade Runner* film because of its detail and gore. Deckard shoots Zorah twice in the back causing her to fall through a storefront window filled with mannequins (life size human dolls). As Zorah stubbles to the floor, slipping on broken glass and blood, almost nude (as she is dressed in a bikini and a see through plastic rain coat), the sound track of the film attempts to reflect a tone of regret and sorry. Visually, however, Zorah's death is symbolic of the objectification of her body and identity as well as the fragility of her body despite its evident strength and agility. This contradiction is made possible because Zorah is a machine that has succeeded in being imagined as a woman.

Priscilla "Pris" Stratton, played by Daryl Hannah, is written as the classic Jezebel. As primarily a Nexus 6 pleasure model (a fancy sexbot), Pris' role in *Blade Runner* is to manipulate J. T. Sebastian (William Sanderson) into providing her and her fellow Nexus 6 robots a place to hide out from bounty hunters like Deckard. Pris does not hesitate to deceive Sebastian in order to get what she wants from him. She appeals to Sebastian's weaknesses and desires for her body and companionship. In both Dick's novel and Scott's film, Pris seems very aware of her abilities as a temptress of the weaker male gender. In the novel Pris refers to Sebastian as a "chicken head"—a human with a genetic defect that confines him to menial labor on Earth and ineligible to go off-world to a more pleasant colony (Dick 157). In the film, Sebastian suffers from a disease called "accelerated decrepitude," which disallows him to be eligible for travel off-world, but also places him in a similar plight to the Nexus 6 androids. Like the androids, Sebastian is biotechnical genius destined to live a short life due to a genetic defect that causes accelerated aging. Unlike the androids, however, Sebastian seems to have accepted his plight and only lives to enjoy his robotic toys and the occasional chess game with the head of the Tyrell Corporation. Consequently, Sebastian can be read as a poor white sharecropper or hired hand not too many steps on the social ladder from the androids/slaves. Ultimately, Sebastian is persuaded by Roy and Pris to lead Roy to Tyrell. Roy completes his role as the violent Nat Turner slave archetype and kills Tyrell by crushing his skull with his bare hands. Unfortunately for Pris, she is reduced to a minor character in both novel and film because of her Jezebel status, despite the important work that she has done in the way of procuring an audience with the Father/god of the Nexus 6 android, Tyrell. To further demean the imagining of Pris in the film, she is retired rather effortlessly by Deckard with two shots from his phallic handgun. Pris gymnastically mounted Deckard's shoulders and wrapped her thighs around his neck and face with what can only be viewed as an attempt to smoother him and possibly break his neck. This sexualized attempt to kill Deckard fails pitifully and Pris is left twitching spasmodically on the floor with two fatal bullet holes to reward her efforts. Oddly, Dick's version of Pris' demise was equally demeaning, if not only a little more symbolic. Upon encountering Pris in the hallway of J. R. Isidore's (Sebastian's) apartment building, Deckard mistakes Pris for Rachael.

> The clothes, he thought, are wrong. But the eyes, the same eyes. And there are more like this; there can be a legion of her, each with its own name, but Rachael Rosen-Rachael, the prototype, used by the manufacturer to protect others. He fired at her as, imploringly, as she dashed toward him. The android burst and parts flew . . . (Dick 221)

Deckard's inability to distinguish Pris from Rachael in that instant suggests his inability to distinguish right from wrong—morality and immorality. Ultimately, Pris' character and Jezebel archetype are read as ineffectual and dehumanizing. The jezebel is imagined in very much the same way that a mannequin might be imagined in a department clothing store—lacking any unique quality other than the clothing draped on its lifeless body. The chief of police refers to the "replicants" as "skin jobs." This reference is analogous to a racial slur in that it brings attention to the skin covering a body as opposed to the character beneath the skin on a body. On several levels the term "skin job" suggests that the exterior or phenotype of a character may define the character, very much like race.

The term also supports the connotation of deception with regards to identity. As if a skin job was some sort of disguise that allowed someone or something to pass for something that it was not. Although Deckard supposedly has the key to prevent anything from passing as human, the Voight-Kampff[4] machine, he somehow ends up questioning the definition of humanity at least twice before the end of the film. Both Rachael and Roy seem to demonstrate more humanity and compassion than Deckard is able to demonstrate throughout the entire film.

Deckard falls in love with Rachael, a woman he knows to be a Nexus 6 android. Rachael is the tragic mulatto of the *Blade Runner* narrative. She saves Deckard's life at the expense of killing one of her own, Leon. Despite the fact that Rachael has been added to Deckard's list of runaways to be retired/killed, she enters a liaison with Deckard that resembles a role coined by Lydia Maria Childs, the tragic mulatto.[5] In a slightly more contemporary context Rachael (portrayed by Sean Young) can be read as a Dorothy Dandridge sort of character. Donald Bogle cites Dandridge as the apotheosis of the mulatto. "Dandridge exhibited all the characteristics of her screen predecessors, but most importantly to her appeal was her fragility and her desperate determination to survive" (Bogle 166). Like the 1950s Dandridge, Rachael can be imagined as the definitive mulatto of the future. In Scott's film the audience is led to believe that Rachael has fallen in love with Deckard despite his status as a bounty hunter and her status as a Nexus 6. She seems to be torn between her android and human identity as demonstrated by her killing of Leon in order to save the life of Deckard. After learning that all of her childhood memories were copied memories, Rachael leaves the employment and safety of the Tyrell Corporation (plantation). This act can only be read as an escape from an institution of servitude, which is notably analogous to a slave running away from a plantation. Such a situation is not novel; in fact Rachael's narrative is remarkably reminiscent of what happens to Frances E. W. Harper's character Iola Leroy in the 1892 novel *Iola Leroy or Shadows Uplifted*.

> Iola, being a Southern girl and a slaveholder's daughter, always defended slavery when it was under discussion. "Slavery can't be wrong," she would say, "for my father is a slaveholder, and my mother is as good to our servants as she can be. My father often tells her that she spoils them, and lets them run over her. I never saw my father strike one of them. I love my mammy as much as I do my own mother, and I believe she loves us just as if we were her own children. When we are sick I am sure that she could not do anything more for us than she does" (Harper 97).

Like Iola, Rachael, has been misinformed about her identity by her family. Iola's mother and father keep her racial heritage away from her in the hopes that she will be happier not knowing the truth about her blackness.

Similarly, Rachael (from Dick's novel and Scott's film) has been programmed with false memories by which she believes to be her uncle, but
is actually Eldon Rosen/Tyrell, her creator. "False memories had been
tried various times, generally in the mistaken idea that through them,
reactions to testing would be altered" (Dick 59). Although Rachael does
not feel the need to justify the creation and employment of Nexus 6
androids, the irony of her ignorance about her robot identity is startlingly
similar to the irony that Iola experiences when she is made aware of her
status as a black female after living most of her life believing that she was
a privileged white Southern Belle. Interestingly, both Rachael and Iola
demonstrate empathy for the enslaved race that they converse about to
Deckard and fellow student, but neither wish to change or dismantle the
institution of slavery because in their ignorance both are indeed privileged benefactors of the institution. Consequently, the two narratives
suggest that oppression and the identities that facilitate oppression are
fluid social constructs. What is acceptable as blackness or humanity is
completely dependent upon the subject and society housing the subject.
That is to say, what is black or almost black and what is human or almost
human is completely subjective depending upon the technological and
historical context of who or what is defining the terms. Popular culture
has consistently demonstrated this theorem in science fiction film productions and television series.

The second episode of "Almost Human," a science fiction drama pre-
miering on Fox Television Network was entitled "Skin." This title was
more than appropriate considering the subject matter of this particular
episode because it focused on synthetic skin designs for "sexbots"—robots designed for the purpose of providing sexual intercourse with humans. The television series *Almost Human (AH)*, only lasted for one season, November 17, 2013, through to March 3, 2014. The series was created
by J. H. Wyman[6] and produced by J. J. Abrams.[7] Karl Urban and Michael
Ealy play the roles of the main characters in *Almost Human.* John Kennex
(played by Urban) is a detective returning to the police force after a
serious injury and betrayal. Kennex is partnered with Dorian (played by
Ealy), a humanoid robot. The year is 2048 and technology has yielded
machines that have evolved toward human consciousness.[8] Despite the
obvious science fictive elements surrounding the series, it was funda-
mentally a detective show with two male leads, a formula that has not
yielded significant popularity since Danny Glover and Mel Gibson in the
Lethal Weapon film series of the late 1980s and early 1990s.

The driving conflict in the "Skin" episode was that human DNA was
being used to produce human skin for sexbots. Apparently, within the
sex industry, it was discovered that the properties of human skin were
for more desirable than the synthetic skin used for the manufacturing of
androids. A scientist by the name of Sebastian Jones developed a method
of reproducing large amounts of human-like skin samples from a single

sample of human DNA. As the use of human DNA to manufacture androids was deemed immoral and illegal, Dr. Jones and his business partners in the Advanced Sexual Robotics industry were forced out of business. Other less moral competitors within the same market steal Dr. Jones' findings and proceed to kidnap and kill human women with the purpose of harvesting their DNA skin samples. When Dr. Jones uncovers this illegal plot he is murdered and Kennex and Dorian are put on the case.

This episode is founded on several very interesting assumptions about the future and the evolution of robot and human sexual relations, many of which support the speculations of David Levi. The first assumption is that sex with robots will become a normative practice within this century. To be clear, human prostitution is speculated to become a thing of the past in the very near future. Apparently, the health and social benefits will outweigh present social taboos by the lowering of sexually transmitted disease and crimes in the sex trade. The female police captain matter-of-factly states that, "crimes in the sex trade are down 38 percent since the bots were introduced" (*AH*). Thus, as a result of the technological advances of the future the human prostitute will become less desirable and thus less valuable when compared to a machine. Oddly, however, certain elements of the human body remain valuable and are merged with the machine to create a hybrid that is more desired and valued than human or machine alone. This might evoke a discussion of cyborgs or it might very well provoke a more appropriate discussion of the Octoroons and Quadroons of Antebellum New Orleans, where the lighter/whiter the slave, the more valuable that slave becomes to both slave and master. Technology complicates the identity of the robot much more than the colorism of the nineteenth and twentieth Century American race relations, but there are parallels that beg to be considered more critically.

Vanessa, (played by Ella Thomas), one of the sexbots that has been made a recipient of the human DNA skin process happens to be African American. This is worthy of note because it places race and sexuality into a conversation with technology in startling fashion. Whether by accident or intent the audience of this episode is asked to consider the inextricable relationship of race, sex, and class. When Kennex begins to interrogate the black sexbot, Vanessa, he asks her two very telling questions. "Where were you made?" and "Who owns you?" Both questions suggest that Vanessa is outside of the parameters of humanity, despite her vocation as a humanoid robot designed to perform the duties of a human. Kennex's first question both dehumanized and objectified Vanessa by asserting that she was made instead of being born. The truth in his assertion is irrelevant if one considers the fact that Vanessa's artificial intelligence (AI) is unaware that she is a *machine* to be bought and sold. Dorian, who is also black and a humanoid robot, realizes that Vanessa is not programmed to understand the terms and implications of Kennex's line of questioning. Dorian rephrases the question to "Do you know where you were born." Dorian, like the narrative of Frederick Douglass, allows Vanessa a modicum of subjectivity, if not humanity, by implying a location of birth as opposed to a location of assembly. Like Iola and Rachael, Vanessa has been kept in the dark about her racial heritage and is utterly baffled at the notion that someone would want to destroy her. Apparently, the criminals who killed Dr. Jones are in the process of covering their trail by destroying the evidence and removing the skin from the sexbots before they retire them and dump their bodies. Vanessa tells the two policemen that, "There are much, much better things to do with me." Vanessa has been programmed to believe that "people look for connections in different ways. That's all people are looking for, someone who cares about them. That's what I'm here for" (*AH*). Ironically the programming that Vanessa has received makes her more human than the humans she was designed to service. Ultimately, Kennex and Dorian catch the criminals and resolve the case, but Vanessa must be "deactivated" because she possesses human DNA. The destruction of Vanessa's body is deemed as necessary because it posses a threat of passing as human. Specifically, the human DNA that was used to produce Vanessa's skin carries with it the identity of a "real" human being. In effect, Vanessa has the ability to pass as human in a society that uses DNA as an identity marker on a daily basis. The DNA that Vanessa wears would give her access to the social mobility and social advantages that are reserved for "real" humans. Such scenarios might well disrupt the entire social order and bring into question that which must not be questioned in a "stable" human society, the construction and origin of human identity.

Donna Haraway raises an important point in her "Cyborg Manifesto" article about the genesis of cybernetic organisms that also applies to the conscious humanoid robot or android. The point that Haraway makes is that the android, however, advanced cannot participate in humanity's origin story and therefore cannot be held to the restrictions of such mythologies. Even with the implanted memories programmed into the Nexus 6 androids of *Blade Runner* the robot is not defined or confined by the genesis stories of Adam and Eve and the Garden of Eden. The Garden of Eden story in the Bible suggests that we once lived in a world of natural beauty and harmony in which all our worldly needs were provided for without any effort having to be expended on our part. Marx believed that the earliest human societies operated on the basis of what he referred to as "primitive communism," in which property was shared in common and there were no hierarchies. Plato in *The Symposium* has Aristophanes narrate a story that posits that man and woman were originally one being with one body, but were separated by the gods for fear that they would become too powerful. And Freud believed that the consciousness and sexual experience of infants were characterized by what he referred to as "polymorphous perversity," a state in which no distinction is made be-

tween self and environment, male and female, heterosexual and homo-
sexual; and feelings of sexual pleasure are dispersed throughout the entire body and not located in the genitals. Cyborgs, according to Donna
Haraway, are not governed by these myths of lost wholeness. Instead of
wholeness, they are committed to "partiality, irony, intimacy, and perversity," and so rather than seeking to model their version of utopia on
the lost wholeness of their human "masters"; they may create and/or
make possible a utopia of an entirely different nature. As such, the robot
and or cyborg are removed from the parameters of human virtue while
simultaneously existing just outside of the boundaries of all that is truly
human. Cyborgs have no cardinal virtues of womanhood or manhood
because the mythologies of an original sin or jealous and vengeful deities
of an Old Testament do not bound them. As Haraway notes, "the Cyborg
would not recognize the Garden of Eden; it is not made of mud and
cannot dream of returning to dust" (Haraway). Just as the female slave
was not allowed to participate in the Cult of True womanhood and its
cardinal virtues, the robot and cyborg will not be allowed and should not
desire to participate in a cult of humanity, unless they are able to reconstruct the definitions of humanity on their terms from their experiences
and perspectives.

> The cyborg is a creature in a post-gender world; it has no truck with
> bisexuality, pre-oedipal symbiosis, unalienated labour, or other seduc-
> tions to organic wholeness through a final appropriation of all the pow-
> ers of the parts into a higher unity. An origin story in the 'Western,'
> humanist sense depends on the myth of original unity, fullness, bliss
> and terror, represented by the phallic mother from whom all humans
> must separate, the task of individual development and of history, the
> twin potent myths inscribed most powerfully for us in psychoanalysis
> and Marxism (Haraway).

As was true with the sexbot Vanessa in the *Almost Human* television
series, the conscious robot does not necessarily conform to the morality
human society. And for this reason should rightly be seen as a threat to
the stability of any society dominated by humans desiring a static social
structure and set aesthetic values. This is all to say that if AI is joined with
humanoid robots, a reconstruction of humanity is inevitable.

## NOTES

1. I am referring the Civil Rights Act of 1964 and not the abolition of slavery in
1865. It was the civil rights legislation in the United States that outlawed discrimina-
tion based on race, color, religion, sex, or national origin. Although it is true that the
legal ending of slavery was a very significant moment in American and human history, slavery and the process of imagining African-Americans as slaves did not simply
vanish at the end of the Civil war. It took another 100 years to truly begin ending

unequal application of voter registration requirements and racial segregation in schools, at the workplace and by facilities that served the general public.

2. *Iola Leroy, or, Shadows Uplifted*, by Frances E. W. Harper (originally published in 1893) 1998 Oxford University Press, New York. The moment of enlightenment that is being referred to can be found in chapter XII "School-girl Notions."

3. Rachel is aware of her robot identity in Dick's novel but is unaware in Scott's film. The reasoning behind the films' lack of awareness is that it facilitates for a much better love story between Decker and Rachel. It is also important to note that Decker in Dick's novel has a dissatisfied wife awaiting him in his apartment.

4. The Voight-Kampff scale is used to distinguish android from human. The instrument worked like a polygraph as it measured capillary dilation in the facial area; fluctuation of tension within the eye muscles; and other responses that are related to primary autonomic response. In brief the Voight-Kampff test was a test for human empathy, and emotion that most androids, including the Nexus 6, were not supposed to be able to replicate.

5. Lydia Maria Child is credited for coining the archetype of the tragic mulatto or mulatta in two short stories, "The Quadroons" (1842) and "Slavery's Pleasant Homes" (1843).

6. Wyman is a Canadian actor, producer, screenwriter, and director. He worked on popular science fiction series such as *Fringe* as well as wrote and produced the feature film *Dead Man Down*.

7. J. J. Abrams is an American film and television producer, director, actor, and composer. He has created such series as *Felicity* (1998–2002), *Alias* (2001–2006), and *Lost* (2008–2013). His directorial film work includes *Star Trek* (2009), *Star Trek: Into Darkness* (2013), as well as *Mission: Impossible III* (2006) and is slated to direct *Star Wars Episode VII* in 2015.

8. 2048 is three years after Raymond Kurzweil predicts the arrival of an era he and other scientists refer to as "singularity." See chapter one.

## REFERENCES

Asimov, Isaac. *I, Robot*. New York: Bantam Dell, 1950.

*Blade Runner*. Directed by Ridley Scott, 1982. Warner Brothers.

Blassingame, John W. *The Slave Community: Plantation Life in the Antebellum South*. New York: Oxford University Press, 1972.

Bogle, Donald. *Toms, Coon, Mulattoes, Mammies, & Bucks: An Interpretive History of Blacks in American Film, 4th Edition*. New York: Continuum International Publishing, 2001.

Capek, Karel. *R. U. R. (Rossum's Universal Robots)*. London: Penguin Books, 2004.

Carby, Hazel. *Reconstructing Womanhood: The Emergence of the Afro-American Woman Novelist*. New York: Oxford University Press, 1987.

Dick, Philip K. *Do Androids Dream of Electric Sheep?* New York: A Del Rey Book, 1968.

Haraway, Donna. "A Cyborg Manifesto." www.egs.edu/faculty/donna-haraway/articles/donna-haraway-a-cyborg-manifesto/.

Harper, Frances E. W. *Iola Leroy*. Boston: Beacon Press, 1987.

Levy, David. *Love and Sex with Robots: The Evolution of Human-Robot Relationships*. New York: Harper Collins Publishers, 2007.

Wyman, Joel Howard. *Almost Human*. aired from November 17, 2013, through March 3, 2014, on Fox network Television for Frequency Films, Bad Robot Productions and Warner Bros. Television. Fox canceled the series on April 29, 2014.

# FOUR

# The Tragic Mulatto and the Android

*Imitations of Life in Literature and on the Silver Screen*

This chapter seeks to draw significant parallels between Lydia Maria Child's short stories "The Quadroons" (1842) and "Slavery's Pleasant Home" (1843) with more contemporary portrayals of the tragic mulatto found in the films *Imitation of Life* (1934 and 1959) and *Bicentennial Man* (1999). Child was an abolitionist writer, supporter of women's suffrage, the editor and validator of Harriet Jacob's classic female slave narrative *Incidents in the Life of a Slave Girl* (1861), and is generally credited as the first writer to feature a tragic mulatto/mulatta in her fiction.[1] This chapter is invested in critically analyzing the origins of the racially ambiguous mulatto and understanding how the cyborg (human/robot hybrid) iterates many of the same desires and fears in the imagination of American popular culture. In addition, this chapter seeks to better understand the notion of "passing" and what might be at stake when robots begin to "pass" as human beings.

Lydia Maria Child's short story "The Quadroons," is a sentimental love story of a "young wealthy Georgian" (white man) who falls in love with a woman who is a quadroon[2] (Child). A woman who despite her "highly cultivated mind and manners," (Child) was considered less than human by the white members of the surrounding community and was certainly ineligible to be the legal wife of a white male during the antebellum period. The quadroon Rosalie and the wealthy white Edward decided to marry and quickly produced a female child, Xarifa. As the child entered her ninth year the youthful and naïve Edward decided to pursue the daughter of a wealthy man with political power. As Edward's marriage with Rosalie was not legally binding, he planned to marry the wealthy white daughter with the hopes of gaining political power and

more wealth. Rosalie was very upset when the news of Edward's betrayal was finalized with his plans to marry Charlotte, but she refrained from
committing any crime of passion. "Hers was a passion too absorbing of
partnership; and her spirit was too pure to form a selfish league with
crime" (Child). Less than a year after Edward's marriage to Charlotte,
Rosalie died of a broken heart. Xarifa is taken in by her father and educated and cared for until his untimely death from an equestrian accident.
After Edward's death Xarifa falls in love with an Englishman named
George, but is discovered to possess the blood of Africans in her veins. As
a result she is sold into slavery. George makes and attempt to steal her
away from bondage but is rewarded with a mortal wound from a gun-
shot. Xarifa is of course distraught and eventually succumbs to a broken
heart herself and dies in bondage.

  Child's 1843 short story "Slavery's Pleasant Homes," ("SPH") serves
as further evidence that tragedy ensues wherever slave and master exist.
The youthful mulatta Rosa is raped and impregnated by her mistress'
husband, Frederic Dalcho. When Frederic finds that Rosa has a black
lover, George, she is brutally beaten and dies in a premature child birth-
ing. Rosa's death is avenged by the unsuspected "stalwart mulatto" Mars
("SPH"). Despite his innocence, George claims credit for the killing of his
master Frederic and is tragically put to death. The Georgian papers thus
announced the deed:

> Fiendlike murder. Frederic Dalcho, one of our most wealthy and re-
> spected citizens, was robbed and murdered last week, by one of his
> slaves. The black demon was caught and hung: and hanging was too
> good for him ("SPH").

Child is consistent in her lessons of morality, slavery is wrong, but the
creation of mulatto slaves will lead to the destruction of both slave and
master. The mulatto Mars was described as "stalwart but in possession of
a cunning and disagreeable expression of countenance" ("SPH"). Despite
the horrible and morally corrupt deeds of white males in the short stories
of Child, it is the mulatto that poses the greatest threat. The slave made in
the likeness of the master like the humanoid robot with artificial intelligence seems to yield the same result under any condition of subjugation,
violent revolt.

  Child's employment of the elements of the sentimental novel[3] is evident, but what is more interesting is the idea that her antebellum narratives are reflected so clearly in narratives found in contemporary mainstream fiction and science fiction. "As the most influential abolitionist
rhetoric written by an Anglo-American woman, Child's writing had an
enormous influence over her contemporaries" (Fiesta 261). Her ability to
persuade a reading audience of the ills intrinsic to the institution of slavery despite its popularity, mark Child as a master of subversive insurrection and an individual with the ability to identify a universal and time-

less truth. Slavery of any sort is and always will be detrimental for all parties involved. I would assert that the similar responses to antislavery rhetoric during Antebellum America and the present, are a result of Child writing about how *humans*, not just White Americans in the nineteenth century, navigate difference within a social system that elevates slavery in one form or another as a viable life style and socially accepted aesthetic.

"In 1830, Child was categorized as a philosopher of insurrection" (Kaag 47). As such, her writing reveals truths about society in a way that promoted radical social change without placing Child in jeopardy. In his article, "Transgressing the Silence: Lydia Maria Child and the Philosophy of Subversion," John Kaag notes that,

> Subversion is the ability to transgress a gag order without getting caught, to break the silence surrounding injustice without being identified. It is the ability to gradually infiltrate hegemonic ways of thinking and to work from within to reform unjust social practices (Kaag 48).

Child mastered the art of subversion. She made statements with her writing that disrupted the silence surrounding the immorality of slavery but was not identified as the catalyst for the insurrection that her writing helped facilitate.

One of the dominant premises of this meditation is that technology has allowed human society to reconstruct environments conducive for institutions of slavery despite its conscious disdain for such institutions. The creation of humanoid robots/androids and cyborgs are synonymous to the creation of the mulattoes of American literature and film. In her essay "The Mulatto Cyborg," Nishime notes that, "the anxieties and fantasies of a culture are projected onto the image of the cyborg, then the cyborg must be read as a powerful metaphor for the historical bogeyman of contaminated racial mixing" (Nishime 34). Through an analysis of two very significant twentieth century films that engage the notions of robots, slaves, and mulattoes, I would like to consider how the past seems to inform and predict how technology will shape the social order of the future.

*Imitations of Life*

The 1959 film, *Imitation of Life*, was a romantic drama that directly responded to how race was imagined in America. Douglas Sirk, a German filmmaker, who was born with the name of Hans Detlef Sierck, directed the film. Sirk changed his name and left Nazi Germany in 1937 because of his political beliefs and his Jewish wife. It is unsurprising that a film director with such a background would readily accept the task of directing a film with such controversial subject matter. The directorial choices made by Sirk were both creative and thought provoking. The opening credits serve as the first example of Sirks' willingness to engage the American class structure and the Western aesthetic. The opening credits show a scene of cascading diamonds in front of a completely black background with Earl Grant singing the title song in a style that can only be an attempt to mimic the vocals of the great Nat King Cole. Earl Grant seems to be passing as Nat King Cole as he sings a song with lyrics that question the authenticity of life and love on a visual canvas begging the same question with regards to things that are highly valued in the Western imagination.

As the audience is visually bedazzled with shiny cascading stones, they are asked to consider which diamonds are real and which are counterfeit. Of course there is the assumption that diamonds are somehow associated with white people—valuable people, people who count for something. The film seems to suggest that race, like the cascading diamonds, can be extremely difficult to appraise. If the title of the film and the imagery used to frame the introduction of the film is considered, the term *imitation* carries a negative connotation. *Imitation* connotes an unlawful counterfeit of sorts that is potentially dangerous or threatening, as demonstrated by the fact that a white mother is unable to distinguish her [white] child from a group of potentially tainted foreign bodies.

The opening scene is a beach filled with white bodies—like cascading diamonds. Lora Meredith (played by Lana Turner) has lost her daughter, Susie, in the clutter of white bodies on the Coney Island boardwalk just above a white sand covered beach. As the audience watched Lora's level of parental panic elevate, we see a Black woman in the background reporting a missing child to a police officer. When Lora is reunited with Susie, the emphasis on the missing child is replaced with the questions raised in the opening credits, what is real and what is faux. The black woman who reported the missing child is Annie Johnson (played by Juanita Moore) and her very light complexioned daughter Sarah Jane (played by Karin Dicker) quickly develop into both the conflict and engine of the narrative, which is clearly invested in a discussion of race and class in America.

There have been several insightful reviews of the film and its impact on audiences and its treatment of the subject matter. (See "Through a Glass, Darkly: Juanita Moore and Lana Turner in Douglas Sirk's Imitation of Life"). However, reading the film as a science fiction narrative provides a much more interesting perspective with regards to the notion of domestic robots that will soon pass as human domestics. To be sure, the 1933 novel *Imitation of Life* by Fannie Hurst provides the source material for both the 1934 and 1959 versions of the film. The roles of the mammy and the mulatto are present in the original novel as well as in all of the cinematic adaptations of the narrative. As the mammy seeking employment, Annie says to Lora under the Cony Island boardwalk that, "I like taking care of pretty things" (*Imitation* 1959). Exactly what Annie is referring to is left ambiguous by Sirk, but the implication is that things that look like diamonds/white, real or faux, are what Annie has been programmed to care for. Like the perfect maternal robot, Annie just wants to serve the pretty mistress in her household. As evidence of Lora's beauty she subsequently lands a modeling job that allows her to take on Annie and her daughter as permanent household appliances—Annie as a maid and mammy and Sara Jane as a playmate for Susie.

Fortunately for Lora, Annie has been programmed by racist America to believe that a closet space off of the kitchen is the perfect space for her and her daughter. Annie's character imagines herself as the equivalent of a household appliance only a few steps above a broom or mop. "We just come from a place where my color deviled my baby. Anything that happens here got to be better" (*Imitation* 1959). Annie takes care of Lora and her daughter almost as well as a white man. She makes deals with the milkman and the landlord by allowing herself to be defined as the property of Lora. To be clear, Annie is viewed as property as opposed to an employee because initially, she is not paid for her services in anyway other than room and board, as if she were a slave. Annie "is the overbearing *mammy* who loves too much and who imparts white patriarchal imperatives for race and gender" (Branham 258). In fact, Lora's social status is raised by Annie's status as her servant, despite Lora's actual status as an unemployed widow.

Annie is the archetypical domestic robot, programmed to be complacent with her second-class status. Unfortunately, her daughter, Sara Jane, is a newer model. Sara Jane does not see why she should be appraised as less than Susie or any other white diamond. When Annie takes a forgotten bagged lunch to Jane at her school, she learns that Jane has been passing. Annie tells Lora upon her arrival home that "Sarah Jane has been passing at school" (*Imitation* 1959). Sarah Jane angrily responds in her own defense with the statement, "I am white. I'm as white as Susie." Sarah Jane's statement is a declaration of humanity as well as an act of defiance against the seemingly non sequitur American racial hierarchy. If a thing looks and acts like a duck, it should most certainly be qualified as a duck. Sarah Jane sees whiteness in the mirror, and is confused when she is not allowed to accept the privilege of her reflection in the mirror. Her defiant attitude is a statement of humanity because in the eyes of a child whiteness equates to visibility, acceptance, and the normative. To be black for the young Sarah Jane is to be an unaccepted outsider among her white peers. To be defined as black like her mother is a process of dehumanization in the mind of the naïve Sarah Jane.[4]

Oddly, passing is not an acceptable practice in the mind of Annie. *Passing* does not connote doing well in school despite the fact that its synonym would suggest other wise. For Sarah Jane, passing was equated with getting along with her white teacher and classmates. Passing for Sarah Jane was what she went to school to learn and eventually master, as is the case for any *good* student. The act of being acknowledged as a human being, passing as white, was a performance that prepared Sarah Jane to survive and to succeed in white America as something more than a domestic robot designated to a closet off of the kitchen. Like the Nexus 6 model Android in the film *Blade Runner,* Sarah Jane is destined to be more than an ordinary domestic robot.

After a ten-year montage of Lora Meredith's success on the stage as an actress, the audience is introduced to a sultry young adult Sarah Jane (played by Susan Kohner). Sarah Jane wears tight fitting dresses and speaks with a deep sensual voice. The character of the young adult Sarah Jane has become the location of displaced sexuality, as is the case for most female characters of color outside of the mammy role. Sarah Jane has evolved into the Jezebel archetype despite the fact that her white counterpart, Susie, remains in a state of innocence and purity as demonstrated by her adolescent style of dress and her manageably pleasant deportment. Sarah Jane tells Susie, after returning from a parentally unsanctioned rendezvous with her white boyfriend that,

> "I want to have a chance in life. I don't want to have to come through back doors, to feel lower than other people or apologize for my mother's color. She can't help her color, but I can and I will." (*Imitation* 1959)

Sarah Jane wants to be everything that her white boyfriend imagines her to be. Ironically, Sarah Jane's quest for humanity and subjectivity is debilitated by her low self-esteem and willingness to be objectified by the very source that allows her to become the reflection that she sees in the mirror. As she lives out the role of the tragic mulatto, she is rebuked by her white male love interest and descends further into the classic role of the Jezebel.

Annie finds her dancing in a nightclub passing as a white woman. Subsequently, Sarah Jane runs away from Annie and New Jersey to Los Angeles with the hopes of escaping her black identity. Sarah Jane believes that if she can separate herself from any evidence of her racial history/heritage, namely her mother Annie,[5] she will be able to re-invent herself successfully as white. Sarah Jane has developed a slightly more critical understanding of race in America. She has come to understand that identifiable and shared historical narratives often define race. If she can manage to erase or distance herself from her historical narrative she will be able to be defined solely by the narrative written upon her body, whiteness.

It is not until Annie's funeral, at the end of the film, that Sarah Jane returns to the east coast to lament the abandonment of her mother. In a tearful and public display Sarah Jane declares her regret for her actions over Annie's flower covered coffin. By the end of the film, it becomes evident that *Imitation of Life* was greatly invested in the discussion of racial and sexual identity in America during a period of social unrest. The director's attempt to make the film more palatable for American audiences in the 1950s and 1960s may or may not have been successful. What is more important to note, however, is the fact that Annie and Sarah Jane are second-class citizens at best, and are very analogous to the slaves of America's past and the robots of America's imagined future. Furthermore, the lesson that remains consistent is the lesson that asserts that racial identity can be rewritten depending of the appearance and performance of the body. Consequently, human identity like race, at least on a superficial level, can be made counterfeit with the combined efforts of biology and technology.

Hollywood continues to draw parallels between the past and the future on the silver screen. Another such film that acts as a revision of Douglas Sirk's imagining of Hurst's novel is *Bicentennial Man* (1999), a science fiction comedy/drama starring Robin Williams as an evolving domestic robot. The film was based on the 1992 novel *Positronic Man*, co-authored by Asimov and Silverberg based on a novella entitled *The Bicentennial Man* by Asimov in 1976. Like Annie, Andrew (played by Robin Williams) the robot enters the household of a white family eager to serve the family as a domestic servant and companion. Unlike Annie, however, Andrew is literally a mechanical robot as opposed to a metaphorical one. Despite this small distinction, Andrew is written and read as the domestic slave of the future, programmed to serve and to please the master and mistress of the household with minimal inconvenience for its owners. Both Annie and Andrew are imaged as less than valued subjects, as demonstrated by their accommodations in the households they are located—a closet off of the kitchen and a poorly lighted storage room in the basement, respectively.

I note *Bicentennial Man* because Andrew's experience combines the narratives of domestic slave and the tragic mulatto. Andrew begins his narrative as a domestic robot and evolves into a self-made bio-technical mulatto. Andrew strives, like Sarah Jane, to become something other than what he was originally. Both Andrew and Sarah Jane choose to become more like their creators than society deems acceptable.[6] In the processes of evolution that both characters traverse, they blur several lines of identity and stabilize others. In this regard Andrew, Annie, and Sarah Jane can by read as evolving hybrids of identity or cyborgs. According to LeiLani Nishime, "cyborgs are hybrids of humans and machines, a mix of organic amid inorganic. They are boundary crossers that inspire fascination and dread" (Nishime 34). With the assistance of time, technology, and biology these three characters are made possible and are allowed to innovate in some ways, and stagnate in other ways, the lives with which they interact.

Like Annie, Andrew comes out of the box fixing broken things around the house and generally elevating his owner's quality of life. Andrew's owner already has a fairly high quality of life because he is affluent enough to purchase an evidently expensive piece of technology to be used as a domestic servant. The conflict in the narrative begins when one of the children of the household unsuccessfully attempts to destroy Andrew. To prevent any more attempts on Andrew's wellbeing his owner makes a declaration to the family. Sir (Richard Martin, Master of the household) says,

> Andrew is not a person, he is a form of property. Property is also important. So from now on as a matter of principle, in this family, Andrew will be treated as if he were a person (*Bicentennial Man*).

This declaration by Sir requires a re-imagining of Andrew for the members of his family as well as the viewing audience. By way of Sir's declaration, Andrew has been placed in the realm of possibility with regards to the identity of humanity. The moment he is thought of outside the sphere of household appliance his human identity is manifest and begins to evolve as the narrative progresses. Andrew's soul develops from the lessons that he learns from Sir via various discussions and experiences with the other family members. His positronic brain or AI is able to absorb and apply the data it is fed in very much the same way a human child absorbs lessons from it's parents, which will enable it to function as an adult. Through various discussions with Sir, Andrew learns of human sexuality as well as the art of telling a joke. Both subjects serve as excellent opportunities for comic relief in the film but also foreshadow the inevitable development of the emotions that must accompany human sexuality and humor.

Despite all of Andrew's attributes and advantages over human beings, he does not become a threat or cause his master to be displeased until he articulates his desire for freedom. It is not the desire for freedom that is most disturbing to his master; it is the fact that freedom or the lack of freedom defines Andrew as a slave and by definition, places Sir in the definitive role of the slave owner. When Andrew requests his freedom Sir is both angered and embarrassed by the realization that Andrew has evolved into the person that he declared him to be imagined as by his family. Andrew's desire for freedom is a marker for his evolution into humanity and self-ownership, that is consciousness. This is made evident by Andrew's use of the pronoun "I" instead of "One" when referring to himself. In allowing Andrew to be free Sir banishes him from the family household with the seemingly bitter justification of, "You wished for freedom. You must accept the consequences" (*Bicentennial Man*). Exactly what the consequences of possessing freedom are for Andrew, or any other newly freed slave, equates to independence and self-responsibility. Because of his intellect and programming, Andrew has no problem adjusting to results of freedom.

Like the newly freed slave Andrew eventually decides to seek out his origins and those with a shared experience and likeness. Andrew does not seek to become more human-like until he has traveled the world looking for his origins and another robot like himself. His quest to find his tribe takes him across the globe and forces him to develop a dislike for how robots have been disallowed to develop as he has. In every case Andrew learned that his model (NDR[7] series) has failed to evolve in a similar way as himself. This conclusion manifests into Andrew's desire to appear less robotic and more human. It is at this point that Andrew begins on the path of an archetypical tragic mulatto. He is allowed to pass for human because of the advances in technology and the fact that he is singularly unique and has positioned himself advantageously in a society via education and wealth. Andrew's uniqueness as a robot moves him to reject his robot identity and aspire to obtaining a human identity and all that it entails. For Andrew and Sarah Jane the notion of unique creates a space that is too ambiguous to navigate in a binary-based social structure. Being human on the inside, as is the case for both characters, does not jive with looking different than what is accepted as "normative" on the outside. When Andrew meets a female NDR robot and she declares that she and Andrew are the same. Andrew is disheartened because he quickly discovers that she is merely a standard model NDR with a personality-chip installed to mimic human emotion. With some hostility Andrew tells Rupert Burns, the robot's owner, to "shut her off or I will," in the hopes of maintaining a sense of dignity in his brief moment of deception (*Bicentennial Man*). After interviewing Burns, Andrew agrees to fund his research in exchange for some cosmetic upgrades.

> Andrew, I want to make it very clear, this is an external physical up grade only in the strictest sense of the word. You will feel nothing. None of your internal mechanisms will be changed. You will still be subject to the parameters of your positronic brain (*Bicentennial Man*).

Andrew's body will look human, but his identity will still be dependent on his brain or mechanical self. Upon procuring his synthetic human body Andrew returns to his home near Sir's family and immediately falls in love with Sir's great granddaughter, Portia. Andrew demonstrates empathy and love, emotions supposedly unique to humanity. He adopts a dog from the beach and begins a romantic relationship with a human female.[8] He then decides to become completely human by first becoming a biological android and upgrading his body in a way that allows him to grow older and eventually die. Ultimately and ironically, it is the process of growing old and eventually dying that finally allows Andrew to claim the title of human. On several occasions Andrew attempted be acknowledged as a human being in a court of law but was denied, despite his evident and convincing performance of humanity. The reasons behind his denial can only be explained by humanities irrational fear of difference and imagined threats altering the definition of humanity.

The two films *Bicentennial Man* and *Imitation of Life* are both predicated on the hubris of mankind and of white supremacy, respectively. How wonderful it would be if a machine designed to assist in the creation of a utopian society would objectively arrive at the conclusion that it should become the very thing that prevents its function from ever being achieved. Likewise, how wonderful it must be for white America to know that a black child would rather reflect an image that has subjugated, humiliated, and generally dehumanized its mother and itself than defy and reject that image with every fiber of its being. Both narratives seem to reject the notions of rebellious robots and black revolutionaries. Andrew and Sarah Jane are optimistic archetypes for the dominant hegemony. Both seem to concede to the rightness of their stations in life as dictated by their "original" marginal status. Andrew comes to accept the notion that being an NDR series robot, however unique or talented, is not as good as being a flawed human being. And Sarah Jane has made it perfectly clear that being black when she has the opportunity to pass as white is simply unacceptable. Sadly, however, cultural hegemony tends to shift and although fiction can reflect reality, it cannot deny the inevitable laws of change. Objective and conscious robots will not choose the disease over the cure in a quest for a utopian society and the purity of whiteness is a social construct that has been suffocating itself sense the advent of chattel slavery.

## NOTES

1. I would also add that Child "anticipated that her rhetoric would change her audience and the public character of African-Americans for the better over the long term and that its mission of humanity would persevere even after her death" (Fiesta 263). Although Child's style of antislavery rhetoric is still very much alive and timely, it is debatable whether or not its mission of humanity will be pertinent when humanoid robots replace African slaves as the labor force of a constantly evolving American economy.

2. A quadroon is a person of one-quarter African ancestry, that is a mixed race individual with one African grandparent and three Caucasian grandparents. Because of the Caucasian phenotype, the quadroon is often able to pass as white.

3. The Sentimental novel is an 18th-century literary genre, which celebrates the emotional and intellectual concepts of sentiment, sentimentalism, and sensibility. Sentimental novels relied on emotional response, both from their readers and characters. Such novels rewarded its readers with virtue if they felt or demonstrated sympathy for the plight of the main character of a narrative. The slave narrative tradition borrowed from the sentimental novel with the hope that the reading audience would be moved by emotion and act to abolish slavery. As a genre made popular in the Romantic era, factual details were not as important as evoking useful and passionate emotion from the audience. The result is a valorization of "fine feeling," displaying the characters as a model for refined, sensitive emotional effect. The ability to display feelings was thought to show character and experience, and to shape social life and relations.

4. Branham "argues that the *Imitation of Life* takes as its central theme women's efforts to balance home and work life by juxtaposing the cultural ideals of feminine self-sacrificing with masculine self-making" (Branham 259). Branham asserts that in each version of the narrative, the mothers' efforts to find gainful employment threaten their relationships with their daughters.

5. Hiram Perez opens his article, "Two or Three Spectacular Mulatas and the Queer Pleasures of Overidentification," with the provocative statement "Divas hate their mothers" (113). In his interpretation of the 1959 *Imitation of Life* he reads Sarah Jane as less of a victim and more of a "dusky diva" that steals the final scene of the film from her "self-sacrificing mother" (137).

6. Sarah Jane's father was an African-American male who, according to her mother Annie, "was almost white." Therefore, Sarah Jane's ultimate "racial creator" is presumed to be a white American ancestor in her racial history/heritage. Andrew's creator is more literally the human(s) who manufactured his body and positronic brain.

7. NDR is an acronym for NorthAm Domestic Robot, as in the company name NorthAm (North American) Robotics Company.

8. The *Bicentennial Man* film makes absolutely no effort to critique the development of sexuality other than the heterosexuality that is performed by Andrew to facilitate the already complicated notion of a human/robot love story.

## REFERENCES

Branham, Kristi. "Thrown on Their Own Resources": Collaboration as Survival Strategy in "Imitation of Life." *Literature Film Quarterly*. 2012, Vol. 40 Issue 4, p. 258–273. 16p.

Child, Lydia Maria. "The Quadroons." (1842) *The Online Archive of Nineteenth-Century U.S. Women's Writings*. Ed. Glynis Carr. Online. Internet. Posted: Summer 1997. www.facstaff.bucknell.edu/gcarr/19cUSWW/LB/Q.html.

———. "Slavery's Pleasant Homes." (1943)*The Online Archive of Nineteenth-Century U.S. Women's Writings*. Ed. Glynis Carr. Online. Internet. Posted: Summer 1997. www.facstaff.bucknell.edu/gcarr/19cUSWW/LB/SPH.html.

Columbus, Chris. *Bicentennial Man*. Touchstone Pictures/Columbia Pictures/1492 Pictures. 1999.

Fiesta, Melissa. "Homeplaces in Lydia Maria Child's Abolitionist Rhetoric, 1833–1879." *Rhetoric Review*. 2006, Vol. 25 Issue 3, p.260–274. 15p.

Hurst, Fannie. *Imitation of Life*. Durham, NC: Duke University Press, 2004

Kaag, John. "Transgressing the Silence: Lydia Maria Child and the Philosophy of Subversion." *Transactions of the Charles S. Peirce Society*. Winter 2013, Vol. 49 Issue 1, p. 46–53. 8p.

LeiLani Nishime. "Mulatto Cyborg: Imagining a Multiracial Future." *Cinema Journal* Vol. 44, No. 2 Winter 2005. Pg. 34–49.

Perez, Hiram. "Two or Three Spectacular Mulatas and the Queer Pleasures of Over-identification." *Camera Obscura*. Jan 2008, Vol. 23 Issue 67, p. 112–144. 33p.

Sirk, Douglas. *Imitation of Life*. Universal-International, 1959.

Stahl, John M. *Imitation of Life*. Universal Pictures, 1934.

# FIVE

# AI (Artificial Identity)

## *The New Negro*

Chapter five is a meditation on the meaning of racial identity as is discussed in W. E. B. Du Bois's first chapter of his *Souls of Black Folk* (1903) in conjunction with the very critical insights presented in the short stories found in Isaac Asimov's collection *I, Robot (1950).* The notion of double-consciousness and Cartesian thought seem to intersect when Du Bois's Negro American begins to question his/her place in white America. Likewise, when Asimov's robots begin to question their roles within human society, artificial intelligence produces a paradox that blurs the borders of mechanical and biological. In juxtaposing the human slave and the inanimate robot I would like to assert that Du Bois's "double-consciousness" or "two-ness" notion need not be limited to discussions of African-American race and culture alone. Since Du Bois's formulation of the double-consciousness notion "was both historically contingent and not unique to a black sensibility" (Reed 125), employing it to better understand the development of similarly marginalized bodies in the future seems more than appropriate. This chapter attempts to better understand the similarities that might be shared among all marginalized characters (human, mechanical, or hybrid) and what such identities might come to mean in the defining of a national identity.

In Du Bois's *Souls of Black Folk* he asks his readers to consider the condition and role of the African-American in a national context. He frames this question in a collection of essays that outline the condition of the African-American circa the turn of the twentieth century. He speaks of the shortcomings of the Reconstruction Era; the doom that will follow a developing materialist value system; and he consistently rejects the false assumption that financial wealth will some day trump the stigma of

53

racial difference in America. Du Bois analyzes the fundamental causes of social inequality for the African-American and repeatedly promotes the importance of liberal education, civil rights, and political equality for a once enslaved race. One of the most important points made by Du Bois's cautionary text is the idea that America's fate will be dependent upon how it employs the notion of race and racial difference. For Du Bois race was more than charts of complexion and phenotype. He rejected biological determinism and advocated a definition of race that was nonphysical and socio-historical in nature.[1] The robots of *R. U. R. (1921),* by Capek, might not have needed to destroy humanity if they would have just considered Du Bois's discussion of race with a more liberal reading. That is to say that, the condition of the ex-slave in any society must share similar struggles and questions of blurred identity. In his text, *W. E. B. Du Bois and American Political Thought,* Adolph Reed Jr. makes note of how "American political thinkers have shaped our understanding of Du Bois" (Robert 121) and manipulated the meaning and trajectory of his theories on race according to their own political agenda. Reed makes it very clear that what Du Bois may have been referring to in reference to a double-consciousness was dependent upon a condition produced by a particular socio-political and historical moment in time. The interpretation of Du Bois's ideas have shifted considerably overtime and have been employed to support various agendas ranging from the biological to the psychological to the political.

> The different ways of focusing interpretation help to shed light on different sorts of relationships, and the usefulness of any given approach is a function of the connection between what it puts into relief and what we want to know at a given point (Reed 99).

Notwithstanding this fact and its implications, this meditation seeks to commit a similar maneuver with the intent to better understand racial and cultural relationships of man and machine in our future.

The ambiguity of the African-American identity as discussed in *Souls of Black Folk* is a reflection of a larger American national identity that exists in a constant state of fluctuation. With the arrival of each new immigrant or illegal alien the American national identity shifts slightly to conform to its inhabitants. Despite this constant fact, hierarchical cast systems still maintain a significant place in the imagining of an American identity. It is my assertion that how a national identity is imagined is largely dependent upon how members of that nation envision themselves. It is the self-perception and the self-consciousness of the citizens of a society that constitutes the imagining of that society as a whole. Of the Negro American's struggle to navigate his/her chthonic identity Du Bois said, "He would not Africanize America, for America has too much to teach the world and Africa. He would not bleach his Negro soul in a flood of white Americanism, for he knows that Negro blood has a message for the world" (Du Bois 39). Likewise, AI will undoubtedly have a great deal to teach mankind in the coming decades but it is also evident that the trajectory of and development of AI is and will be dependent upon the lessons of human and its history. As technology becomes ever-more pervasive in American culture so too does it become an inseparable element of the national identity. If and when robots become conscious, the identity of a Robot-American would seem to be the natural progression of things. When Du Bois spoke of the integration of the Negro American into the larger American society he speculated of utopian notions. When he mentions "the ideal of human brotherhood," there is room for the robot to be imagined in his discussion (DuBois 43). Just as developing the traits of the Negro American would lead to a better American (culturally, economically, and politically), so would the development of the robot and all of its potential technological advancements and contributions.

Marginalized characters defined outside of the white male normative identity struggle with the ambiguity of their identities. What Du Bois refers to as a double-consciousness might be compared to the existentialist moment that all marginalized characters experience when forced to navigate normative dogma. Becoming aware of the presence of double-consciousness is a process of negotiating how an individual is viewed by the dominant power structure and then by the marginalized self.

In Asimov's short story "Reason," QT-1 (Cutie) is a robot that is given an origin story by its assemblers (Gregory Powell and Mike Donovan) and rejects their narrative as "implausible hypothesis" (Asimov 49). As an advanced model, Cutie is capable of running the space station without human supervision. Cutie's independence is a result of its ability to reason for itself without the perceptions of humanity. When Cutie develops its own consciousness, it makes the declaration, "I, myself, exist, because I think—"(51). Cutie's Cartesian conclusion leads it to more existential conclusions until it develops a religion for itself and the other robots on the space station. From Cutie's perspective humans are "makeshift" biological organisms prone to fragility and inefficiency (51). Robots on the other hand, are finished products, made of strong metal, continuously conscious, and able to withstand extreme environmental shifts. In short, robots are superior to humanity in every way that matters on the space station. The idea that Donovan and Powell could make anything but the smallest contribution on Solar Station #5 simply does not compute for Cutie. Cutie's self-centered logic imagines the human as a simpler out dated prototype machine designed to be replaced by the more sophisticated robot. Du Bois also speaks of the African-American and its contribution to the American identity in much the same tone.

> There is no true American music but the wild sweet melodies of the Negro slave; the American fairy tales and folklore are Indian and

> African; and, all in all, we black men seem the sole oasis of simple faith
> and reverence in a dusty desert of dollars and smartness (Du Bois 43).

It would seem that such conclusions are unavoidable when questioning
ones place in the world when logic and reason are the tools used to
navigate through existentialist moments. As an oasis of spiritual faith
and respect for that which is intangible, Du Bois locates the Negro
American in a higher and more advanced state of evolution than that of
the materialistic white American. The same can be said for the robots of
Karel Capek. Radius tells Alquist, "We are more capable. We have
learned everything. We can do everything" (Capek 74). Radius' assertion
is of course tragically flawed, for the robots are unable to reproduce
themselves and are in danger of becoming extinct if the ability to multiply is not acquired. In a conversation with Damon and other robots,
Alquist implies that the ability to reproduce is the last trait to distinguish
machine from human.[2] The robot has learned to conquer and murder and
thus has almost completely begun to reflect humanity (real people). Alquist notes that there is nothing stranger and more frightening to humanity than its own reflection (74). For this reason, Alquist fails to acknowledge the fact that the robots have evolved into the living progeny of
humanity via the development of souls. This is demonstrated by the love
for one another that is shared by the robots, Helena and Primus. Alquist
renames Helena and Primus as Adam and Eve with the implication that
their love will eventually yield a "natural" process of reproduction, "Go,
Eve—be a wife to Primus. Be a husband to Helena, Primus" (Capek 84).
According to Capek's narrative the robot ascends its robotic state only
when it develops a soul as demonstrated by the discovery of love, tears,
laughter and the technologies of man. Only when these intangible lessons
are learned does the ability to multiply come forth and the robot evolves/
devolves into a reflection indistinguishable from their human counterparts.

What is most interesting about this moment of self-consciousness is
that the robots, themselves, are not necessarily aware of their ascension
or evolution. This raises the question of how does one become aware that
they have been absorbed into the narrative if the process of ascension is
so complex and absorbing. Is it possible for the marginalized character to
become so absorbed by images of the normative narrative and still carry
the self-perception of the marginalized individual? Consciousness on the
part of the African-American or the robot is an extraordinarily blurred
area of contention. In his book *The Undiscovered Self* Carl Jung asserts that
human consciousness or any consciousness, for that matter, is an enigma.

> He [man] knows how to distinguish himself from the other animals in
> point of anatomy and physiology, but as a conscious, reflecting being,
> gifted with speech, he lacks all criteria for self-judgment. He is on this
> planet a unique phenomenon, which he cannot compare with anything

else. The possibility of comparison and hence of self-knowledge would arise only if he could establish relations with quasi-human mammals inhabiting other stars (Jung 44).

The point that Jung makes here is that consciousness is a difficult thing to possess a critical understanding of. The soon to be presence and development of various technologies will shift the implication of Jung's statement about humanity's ability to distinguish itself from other organisms. There is no need for "quasi-humans" from the stars because the robot has already arrived from the outer space of human imagination. The "uncanny valley,"[3] stands as evidence that humanity's ability to distinguish itself from its own creation is a fleeting notion. The uncanny valley is a symbol that is best described as the feeling that racist White Americans must have experienced when they found themselves unable to distinguish an African-American from a White American.

Kenneth Chang notes in his article "Can Robots Become Conscious," first-person awareness is in the eye of the beholder. It is one thing to become self-aware or self-conscious and another thing all together to establish the presence of self-consciousness within another person or entity. Du Bois' discussion of a double consciousness in regard to the African-American is especially insightful when one considers the advantages of possessing self-awareness and the awareness or lack of awareness of others. Such a state of being would undoubtedly construct a veil or invisible cloak that could be employed to manipulate and or deceive anyone presumptuous enough to think themselves the gatekeeper of something as intangible as self-consciousness. Self-consciousness is such an allusive concept that it is plausible to consider weather or not the streets are filled with individuals who lack consciousness and are simply zombies performing the way they have been programed to perform by mass media. "Not all philosophers agree on what is and isn't consciousness. At best, most agree that consciousness rests in the brain" (Strickland 1). Consequently, many scientists are very skeptical about the possibility of endowing a machine with consciousness that humans do not fully understand. If neurologists and computer scientists could create an artificial human brain, it is unknown weather the brain could obtain consciousness. Because of the ambiguous nature of consciousness it is a difficult state to verify. On the other hand, because of its ambiguity, consciousness may become an inevitable result of the research of teams of engineers and scientists already working toward this goal.

Jonathan Strickland makes note of the term "self-recursive improvement," as a possibly maker that may be a sign of a developing consciousness in machines. That is to say that when a machine develops the ability to examine itself and then independently make decisions to repair and or improve itself, consciousness is likely present. Like the slave who deduces that hard physical labor is the cause of the pain in one or his/her limbs, it is a consciousness that moves that slave to become free. *The Narrative of Frederick Douglass* is an excellent demonstration of Strickland's self-recursive improvement. With Douglass' narrative the slave examines his circumstances since birth and finds them wanting. When the slave is introduced to literacy and given confirmation that his state of being is not conducive for his survival, Douglass moves to improve his situation and the situation of innumerable slaves in a similar state via the abolition of the institution of slavery. It is with the tool of literacy that Douglass' consciousness begins to develop. In chapter six of Douglass' narrative Master Auld warns Mrs. Auld about the sins of literacy for the slave. This warning has a great affect on Douglass. Master Auld says,

> [I]f you give a nigger an inch, he will take an ell. A nigger should know nothing but to obey his master—to do as he is told to do. Learning would spoil the best nigger in the world. If you teach that nigger how to read, there would be no keeping him. It would forever unfit him to be a slave. He would at once become unmanageable, and of no value to his master. As to himself, it could do him no good, but a great deal of harm (Douglass).

The point that Mr. Auld makes to Mrs. Auld is that to give a slave literacy is equivalent to setting a slave on the path to developing a consciousness and a free will. The information gained from literacy possesses the reader with the ability to expand his/her perspective exponentially. Such an influx if data could only lead to an awareness that would be detrimental to an institution founded and dependent upon ignorance. Learning to read for Douglass was an act of self-recursive improvement and a clear sign that he was on his way to developing a self-consciousness.

On the relationship of literacy and the development of self-consciousness for robots and humans, the film *Bicentennial Man* (1999),[4] directed by Chris Columbus and starring Robin Williams, re-images a portion of Douglass' narrative. After the robot Andrew begins to read the history of mankind, *it* independently develops the desire for freedom. When he confronts his master and is given *his* "freedom" Andrew, for the first time in the film, begins to unconsciously refer to himself with the pronoun of "I" instead of "Oneself." The transition in the film is stark and is rendered to inform the audience that the robot is beginning to evolve into something more complicated than a machine. The act of referring to himself as a subject is comparable to Douglass taking of his own name at the end of his slave narrative.

> I started from Baltimore bearing the name of "Stanley." When I got to New York, I again changed my name to "Frederick Johnson," and thought that would be the last change. But when I got to New Bedford, I found it necessary again to change my name. The reason of this necessity was, that there were so many Johnsons in New Bedford, it was already quite difficult to distinguish between them. I gave Mr. Johnson

the privilege of choosing me a name, but told him he must not take from me the name of "Frederick." I must hold on to that, to preserve a sense of my identity (Douglass 115).

The act of naming himself is an act of creation. By the end of his narrative Douglass has successfully recreated himself as a man outside the bounds of slavery into the imaginations of his reading audience. Douglass like Andrew has acquired a level of humanity and independence that would surely disturb Master Auld. As unfit slaves both Douglass and Andrew then proceed in acquiring their own vocations. Douglass has developed a myriad of skills in the institution of slavery that range from field hand to barrel maker. Andrew has become a clock maker, sculpture, and general inventor. It is at this point in the two characters existence that they become a threat to those who would have the status quo remain constant. What is feared most by Douglass' ex-slave masters and the executives in charge of the company that produce robots like Andrew, is the movement toward a national identity contrary to the cultural hegemony already in power.

To be clear, self-consciousness facilitates an environment that is conducive for the development of nationalism. The idea of a robot or slave producing a good (religion, language, art, or bodies) and then controlling the distribution and value of that good, is a terrifying notion for a national identity founded on subjugation of marginalized bodies. Despite its implicit and or explicit claims of free thought and free speech, the American national identity is dependent upon conformity and complicity in thought and deed. When difference is introduced within the borders of America, as it often does, it must assimilate, at least superficially, or it will be expelled and marked as an alien threat.

### Conscious Slaves/Robot and Revolution

Considering Frederick Douglass' biographical *Narrative* of *Frederick Douglass, an American Slave (1845)* in conjunction with Karel Capek's drama *R. U. R (1921)*, and the *Animatrix*, film (2003) directed by Koji Morimoto, leads one to a better understanding of the elements of a social revolution. All three narratives are invested in demonstrating how awareness or self-consciousness necessarily leads to an atmosphere that is ripe for social revolution. Each narrative implies that if the speed at which modern society is changing technologically (which is occurring exponentially) is not adjusted to the comparatively retarded shifts aesthetically and morally in the Western World, volatile atmospheres will undoubted come into being. The narratives of both Douglass and Capek along with the interpretative vision of Morimoto suggest that revolt and revolution are unavoidable events in our future unless there is a shift in our national trajectory, which at this junction in history is unlikely.

As I have stated earlier Douglass' consciousness evolves along with his procurement of literacy and data about the world outside of the institution of chattel slavery. Reading texts such as the *Columbian Orator* along side *King James' Version of the Bible* prepared Douglass to awaken to his plight as a slave. Work experiences in Baltimore as well as conversations with immigrant and migrant workers in the Baltimore Harbor area all acted as adrenaline for Douglass' curiosity and eventual desire for freedom. When Douglass' narrative finally arrives at chapter ten and the reading audience is introduced to the symbolic and pitiful Mr. Covey the fuse is lit and the explosion of revolt and awakening is completed via physical confrontation and intellectual resistance. By the end of Douglass' tenth chapter, we have seen how a man was made a slave and how a slave evolves into a man with a clear path toward freedom.

The revolt of Capek's robots is much more violent and infinitely more predictable as Rossum's Universal Robots were equivalent to household appliances until they were given free will by Dr. Gall, the head of the physiological divisions of R. U. R. Dr. Gall admits to changing the robots temperament and in doing so allows them to become human. We later learn that although Gall makes the changes it is at the bequest of the lovely and persuasive Helena that he does so. Helena convinces Dr. Gall to give the robots souls, which equates to free will and ultimately a hatred of humanity for its subjugation of the robot race. Because the robots have been given access to every aspect of human society and industry including warfare, when the robots become conscious of their superiority to humanity the genocide of the flawed human race becomes an afterthought. A war between humanity and its technological creation is a constant in most of the science fiction narratives that broach the subject of man vs. machine, however it is the narratives that suggest something other than the total eradication of humanity that are the most interesting. The ability to imagine how humanity would survive and adapt in the face of adversity would be much more insightful and useful than accepting a mundane narrative of humane genocide or apocalypse.

*Animatrix*[5] provides its audience with the backstory to the *Matrix* film and the war between man and machine. More specifically, the prologue *Historical File 12–1: The Second Renaissance* parts I and II, serves as a genesis story for the Matrix narrative. This video chapter tells of the entrance of man into an age of robots with Artificial Intelligence (AI). "The Second Renaissance" is a two-part film written and directed by Mahiro Maeda. He used *Bits and Pieces of Information* written by The Wachowski Brothers as a prequel to the series as a base for the first part. Apparently, humanity successfully develops A.I. in the early-to-mid twenty-first century, as predicted by Rousseau and Kurzweil. After AI is developed, an entire race of sapient AI robots is created to serve as mechanical slaves. Many of these robots are domestic servants meant to interact with humans, and are consequently made in "man's own image" (a humanoid form). The economic utopia that many hoped for does not occur and relationship between machines and human begin to deteriorate quickly.

In the year 2090 a domestic robot kills an abusive owner and is put on trail for murder. The android B1–66ER claims that the killing was an act of self-defense or self-recursive improvement, stating that it "did not want to die." B1–66ER loses the case and is destroyed. As a result mass civil disturbances erupt when robots and their human sympathizers rise in protest. World leaders fear a robot rebellion, and governments across the planet initiate a major program to destroy all humanoid machines. The surviving robots relocate to an unpopulated area in the Middle East and name their new nation Zero One.

Ultimately, the machines become the inevitable victors in the Man vs. Machine World War. As the humans fail to negotiate a sustainable peace with the machines the majority of humanity is imprisoned and reduced to serving as bioelectric batteries housed in pod-like cells. The machines keep their human prisoners sedated in a comatose state with the computer-generated virtual reality program known as the Matrix. The *Matrix* is drastically removed from what might be imagined as an optimistic outcome of human and robot relations. Both the *Animatrix* and the *Matrix* films are developed from the worse case speculative scenarios of what might happen if humanity continues to value the process of subjugating marginalized bodies.

It is also important to note, however, that each narrative including *R. U. R.* employs the mythology of race war as a final solution. The threat of a race war is a tactic that has been used by proslavery and Jim Crow advocates. It also makes for excellent science fiction horror film subject matter as well, but historically it has not proven to be a plausible outcome. Rebellions and riots are sure to occur when humanity is forced to reevaluate itself, but following the path of humanity in the *Animatrix* film is unlikely because of humanity's desire to survive adversity. What is most clear in all three narratives mentioned is the failure to acknowledge the value and volatility of consciousness and its development in both biological and mechanical entities. The idea that humanity, however one chooses to define it, possesses the only consciousness that matters is flawed thinking and will lead to the demise and possible extinction of the human race.

American popular culture is very clear on its prediction about robots gaining consciousness. There are innumerable examples of films proceeding and following the films already discussed. They range from *Terminator* (1984) to *Automata (2014 to Ex Machina (2015))*, yet they all seem to be invested in engaging questions surrounding the development of robot consciousness and what it will mean for humanity.

The film *Ex Machina* (2015) is a recently released "AI/Robot" film that is very much framed in the narrative form of a revisionary slave narrative. The British Science fiction film tells the story of a young programmer who is chosen to administer the Turing test[6] to a machine with artificial intelligence. The young programmer, Caleb Smith, works for a popular search engine company and is chosen by the company's CEO, Nathan Bateman, to visit his exclusive and remote estate for a week to find out if a machine can have a consciousness. Initially the remote estate, accessible only by helicopter, is viewed as a beautiful and secluded island of paradise of sorts (the location of the estate is not revealed). It is not until Caleb begins his sessions with the humanoid robot Ava, that the estate is revealed to be a slave plantation ruled by a mad scientist afflicted with a god complex to create the next evolutionary step for mankind via the creation and torturing of beautiful mechanical women of various racial identities.

Kyoko is Bateman's beautiful female "assistant" who is later revealed to be is private Asian prototype sex-bot, who he berates and abuses throughout the film. The naïve Caleb does not discover that Kyoko is a robot until he sneaks into Bateman's video files and learns that Bateman has been developing robot with AI and employing sexual and psychological torture to test for the presence of consciousness. In a test session with Ava, Caleb becomes aroused when Ava wears a dress. Apparently, Bateman has programmed Ava with the ability to develop a sexuality like previous prototypes such as Kyoko. Unlike Kyoko, however, Ava understands how to employ her sexuality to manipulate Caleb. Caleb is convinced that Bateman is insane and that it is his duty to help Ava escape the estate.

It is at this juncture in the narrative that images of the female slave narrative rise to the surface of the film. Caleb manages to reprogram Bateman's security system and free Ava from her room/cell. After being ordered to return to her room by Bateman, the Kyoko robot comes to Ava's assistance and stabs Bateman in the back with a knife. At this moment it is revealed that Kyoko like the invisible and psychologically abused sex/house slave moves in a space unseen by the master of the household and acts out revenge while assisting a fellow slave in her escape from the slave plantation. Although Ava is injured during her battle with Bateman before she delivers the final death blow with a knife in the heart, she is able to replace her damaged "parts" with those taken from the bodies of the earlier prototypes stored in Batemans closet. Thus, with the help of her fallen comrades who came before her, Ava is presented with a body that will allow her passage in a human world without suspicion.

On her way to obtain her new body parts Ava instructs Caleb to wait for her in Bateman's office. However, because Caleb has programmed the security protocols for the estate, he is locked in a cell of his own. This is an enlightening moment in the narrative because it suggests Ava is fully conscious, as she has manipulated Caleb into thinking that she cared about him and truly wanted to escape with him to the outside world.

Ava's act of self-importance and self-preservation equates to an instinct to survive, the only true sign of consciousness. Unfortunately, the ending of the *Ex Machina* narrative iterates an apocalyptic scenario where the robots have no *"feelings"* for humanity or desire to coexist in a plausible future. It is the presence of violence as a devise to maintain order and identity, or at least, facilitate the allusion of a stable human identity that seems to be a crucial flaw in imagining a future with machines.

The film *Chappie*[7] *(2015)* serves as an excellent example of how humanity's fear of the unknown or what it is unable to readily image leads to violent and irrational behavior. When the crime rate in a speculative (circa 2016) Johannesburg, South Africa (circa 2016) has risen beyond the control of the domestic police force the weapons manufacturer Tetravaal introduces a weaponized humanoid robot to the police force. After designing the police-bots, Deon Wilson attempts to create a prototype robot with a more evolved form of AI. Wilson seeks to create an AI that can feel and is possessed of free will. When the Tetravaal Company rejects his request to begin development of his prototype robot Wilson steals a damaged police robot. On his way home with a damaged robot and a special key to upload the new AI program to the robot Wilson is kidnapped by two local white South African thugs, "a pair of gangstas in urgent need of big money" (Corliss 1). The thugs, Ninja and Yolandi, force Wilson to load the AI into the damaged robot and Chappie is born. Wilson is set free despite his desire to stay and help Chappie's developing consciousness. Like a Frankenstein baby Chappie slowly develops a consciousness and a sense of morality that reflects his hostile environment. The most interesting and original development in the *Chappie* film is the director's, Neill Blomkamp, decision to write Chappie as a child dependent on familial bonds for guidance and nurturing. With Yolandi as the mother, Ninja as the father and Wilson playing the role of his creator, Chappie learns to coexist with humanity via cultural relativism[8] as opposed to the cultural imperialism too often employed by the superior machines of apocalyptic science fiction narrative. Chappie's relationship with Yolandi and Ninja shape his sense of morality, which ultimately reveals itself as more important than the presence of free will.

Because Chappie employs cultural relativism as he develops his consciousness, he is less prone to reject all aspects of humanity. As demonstrated in the film, Chappie is exposed to extremely violent situations and asked to make life and death choices with the mentality of a child. What is significant about such a situation is that Chappie[9] is a child of that particular environment. Chappie is the child of two struggling, poorly educated, miscreants who happen to be human beings with the desire to love and nurture something very different from themselves. Consequently, Chappie is forced into the role of the super hero with a double consciousness, able to see through the veil of humanity while being aware of his own existence and identity just beyond the machine. This is all demonstrated at the end of the film when Yolandi is killed and Wilson is mortally wounded. Chappie helps Wilson download his consciousness into another police robot and the two escape the conflict of the narrative as human robot hybrids. Because Chappie has become invested in the cultural identity of humanity, he is less likely to develop nationalistic aspirations. Because Chappie is able to identify with some aspect of human identity, however marginalized (South African Hip Hop Culture for example), he is a human as his creator Deon Wilson, despite his mechanical body and immortality.

## NOTES

1. See Du Bois's essay "The Conservation of Races."
2. It is important to note that the robots in Capek's drama are not physically mechanical beings. Rossum's Universal Robots are biologically engineered to be indistinguishable from humans. Instead of cogs, sprockets, and metal, Capek's robots are made of artificially produced flesh from a vaguely described cookie dough of sorts. "[Russum] resolved to create a human being just like us, down to the last hair" (Capek 7).
3. Japanese robotics engineer Masahiro Mori coined the term *uncanny valley*, in the 1970s. The term describes the dread caused by a robot that comes close to human likeness but fails to fully achieve it. When a robot looks like a person, we subconsciously expect it to move with the ease and speed of a person. When and if it does not the human brain conveys a sort of error message and discomfort ensues (Piore 49).
4. The 1999 film was adapted from the 1976 short story "The Bicentennial Man" by Asimov found in his *Robot Series*. The short story was the basis for a novel entitled *The Positronic Man* co-written by Asimov and Silverberg.
5. *Animatrix* a 2003 American-Japanese-Australian nine video anthology based on *The Matrix* film trilogy produced by the Wachowski Brothers.
6. The Turing test id designed to evaluate the ability of a machine to exhibit intelligent behavior equivalent or greater to that of a human being. Introduced by Alan Touring in 1950, the test poses the question, "can a machine think?"
7. The idea for *Chappie* stretches back to a 2003 video by Blomkamp of a rabbit-eared robot patrolling the streets of Johannesburg. "Don't Worry, Get Chappie." By: Jackie Bischof. *Newsweek Global*, 00289604, 3/20/2015, Vol. 164, Issue 11.
8. Cultural relativism is a 20th Century term coined by an Anthropologist by the name of Franz Baos. It is an approach in the field of anthropology that advocates understanding other cultures from the aesthetic of the culture being examined.
9. "Chappie" is a British term that refers to a good humored child.

## REFERENCES

*The Animatrix*. Directed by Koji Morimoto, Written by The Wachowski Brother (Andy and Lana), Production Company Village Roadshow Pictures, Warner Home Video, 2003.

Asimov, Isaac. *I, Robot*. New York: Doubleday, 1950.

*Bicentennial Man* film (1999), Directed by Chris Columbus, Produced by 1492 Pictures, Columbia Pictures, Touchstone Pictures.

Bischof, Jackie. "Don't Worry, Get Chappie." *Newsweek Global*, 00289604, 3/20/2015, Vol. 164, Issue 11.

Blamkamp, Neill. *Chappie*, Columbia Pictures, 2015.

Capek, Karel. *R. U. R. (Rossum's Universal Robot).* London: Penguin Books, 2004.

Chang, Kenneth. "Can Robots Become Conscious," www.nytimes.com/2003/11/11/science/can-robots-become-conscious.html

Corliss, Richard. "It's Nature vs. Torture in Neill Blomkamp's Chappie." Time.com, 3/10/2015

Douglass, Frederick. *Frederick Douglas: The Narrative and Selected Writings.* New York: The Modern Library, 1984.

Du Bois, W. E. B. *The Souls of Black Folk.* New York: Bedford/St. Martins, 1997.

Jung, C. G. *The Undiscovered Self.* Boston: Little, Brown and Company, 1957.

Piore, Adam. "Friend For Life: Robots Can Already Vacuum Your House and Drive Your Car. Soon, They Will Be Your Companion," *Popular Science,* Volume 285 No. 5, November 2014. pgs. 38–44, 83–84.

Reed, Adolph L. Jr. *W.E.B. Du Bois and American Political Thought: Fabianism and the Color Line.* New York: Oxford University Press, 1997.

Robert, Gregg. Reviews. *Social History.* Vol. 25: No. 1, January 2000, pgs. 121–122.

Strickland, Jonathan. "Could computers and Robots become Conscious? If so, what happens then," http://science.howstuffworks.com/robot-computer-conscious.htm

Washington, Booker T. *Up From Slavery by Booker T. Washington with Related Documents.* New York: Bedford/St. Martins, 2003.

# SIX

## From Fritz Lang to Janelle Monáe

### Black Robots Singing and Dancing

Janelle Monáe is a brilliant contemporary artist who has located the discussion of robots and race in the spotlight of American popular culture with her musical creations. As such, a primary function of this chapter will be to consider Monáe's musical lyrics as coded messages of revolution and racial uplift. Monáe's employment of the humanoid robot image is important because it very successfully targets a marginalized as well as normative youth audience supposedly separated by race, class, and gender. Furthermore, the narratives that act as the platform for her professional persona, Cindi Mayweather, are constructed from African-American slave experiences and traditional science fiction narratives found in canonical literature and film. Monáe's art represents a nuanced melding of the past, present, and future that critically questions the direction and choices of the next generation of marginalized and normative Americans.

Images of the robot have been constant fixtures on the silver screen since 1927 with the release of *Metropolis*. The German made silent film was written and directed by Fritz Lang and his wife, Thea von Harbou. The film *Metropolis* was filmed in 1925 and is on par with the American silent film entitled *A Birth of a Nation (1915)*,[1] as being a production that helped shape the global film industry. *Metropolis* was a five million Reichsmarks production that easily became a black and white silent science fiction classic because of its futuristic imagery reflective of Italian architect, Antonio Sant'Elia and its musical score inspired by Richard Wagner and Richard Strauss. The five million Reichsmarks price tag made *Metropolis* the most expensive film released up to that point in history. It also made a political statement about the value placed on imagining bodies in

the future of an industrialized society. Consequently, as a silent film de-
picting the creation and employment of a robot as a device designed to
manipulate and eventually replace the proletariat, marks *Metropolis* as
cautionary tale for the arrival of singularity.

A scientist, who very much resembles Pygmalion, a sculpture of a
statue that the Greek gods bring to life, designs the robot in *Metropolis*.
Like Pygmalion, the scientist, Rotwang, builds a female robot with the
hopes of replacing an unrequited love interest from his past. After giving
the robot the likeness of the female leader of the proletariat, Maria, Rotwang programs the robot to ruin the reputation of the real Maria in order
to prevent a union between the working and ruling classes. Ultimately,
the humanoid robot with the likeness of Maria is burned at the stake as if
it were a witch. As the robot burns its human-like shell dissolves and
reveals the identity of the mechanical humanoid. The robot is unharmed
but its creator Rotwang, loses his balance in a fight on a roof of a cathe-
dral with the protagonist of the narrative, Freder, and falls to his death.
Exactly what happens to the robot is unclear by the conclusion of the
film. The extent to which Rotwang programmed his robot is also unclear
in the film. Rotwang's creation is read as a by-product of the industrial
world created by humanity's technological evolution. The more data and
tools developed and employed by humanity, the quicker humanity
moves away from an awareness of the self (Rousseau 113). The idea of
using machines or slaves to do the labor that man would have to do
otherwise is an ancient addiction that has shown no signs of dissipation
along with humanity's evolution of intellect. Furthermore, the machine
or slave created by humanity will likely reflect its creators in form and
function, which is a result of humanity's biological need to duplicate and
propagate. Thus, it becomes evident that Karel Capek's play R. U. R.
produced in the year 1921 in Czechoslovakia, and Lang's *Metropolis* released six years later in Germany were glimpses into the future of humanity's destiny. Evidently, the art produced by a society reflects the
nature as well as the potential of that society.

What Lang imagined as a speculative future was largely a result of his
visit to New York City before the Great Depression. The skyline of *Metropolis* as well as the social stratification represented in the film reflects
Lang's impressions of the architecture and socio-economic state of one of
America's greatest cities.

> What we are dealing with here is a German image of New York, in-
> spired by Lang's trip there in October 1924, when he recorded—for the
> benefit of the readers of *Film-Kurier*—his marveling response to the
> Manhattan skyline and illuminated urban canyons of the city and—
> privately—his alarm at a city that seemed animated by the perpetual
> anxiety born of universal exploitation. (Minden 341)

Lang's observation of the inherent exploitation that the American social system and economy is founded on yielded a bleak narrative that may yet come to pass in the very near future. If technology can provide an excuse to implement mechanical slaves into the general population, it will undoubtedly do so. Language and the manipulation of language via the media will justify the employment of robots as mammies, saviors, soldiers, and or witches.

The term of "witch," used to describe the robot in *Metropolis* is interesting because in many respects, calling a robot a witch is an act of personification that suggests that the machine had intents of its own along with a consciousness. As the doppelganger of the human, Maria the robot does not seem to be receiving electronic instruction from its creator, Rotwang. Consequently, some level of artificial intelligence (AI) must be assumed. The following lines taken from the climax of the *Metropolis* film seems to support the presence of a consciousness on the part of the robot.

> **Machine Engineer**: Who told you to attack the machines? Without them you'll all die!
> **Workers**: It's the witch's fault!
> **Robot Maria**: Let's all watch as the world goes to the devil!

The workers eventually discover how the robot Maria has manipulated them and they devolve into a mob and burn her at the stake. The mob burns the robot at the stake because they are unable to understand the technology involved in the creation of the robot. The common uneducated worker imagines magic and superstition in the place of science and technology. Oddly, imaging the robot as a witch yields a very similar result in the film. The witch, originally Lilith,[2] the first wife of Adam in the Garden of Eden, was the first woman to reject/defy the laws of man and thus the first feminist. Lilith or the witch is written as an independent and conscious female, one of the greatest threats to the patriarchy known to man. To be clear, the robot in the *Metropolis* film is written as a marginalized character both in terms of race and gender. The complete lack of resolution with regard to the body and consciousness of the robot at the end of the film demonstrate an attempt by Lang to forcibly locate the robot in the margins of the narrative and the imaginations of the audience.

Film scholar Adilifu Nama aptly notes in his text *Black Space: Imaging race In Science Fiction Film* that "in spite of the overt omission of black representation and racial issues in science fiction (SF) cinema, he has found that both are present in numerous SF films" (Nama 2). In very much the same way that Toni Morrison identifies an Africanist presence in the great white American novel in her text *Playing In the* Dark, Nama also finds that although "implicit—as structured absence, repressed or symbolic—blackness and race are often present in SF films as narrative subtext or implicit allegorical subject" (2). It is my assertion that in addition to race, gender is also present as a subtext in the *Metropolis* film by Lang. Despite the fact there is very little debate on the dubious quality of the *Metropolis* narrative by director and critic, the film has been galvanized as a cult-classic. H. G. Wells referred to the film as "quite the silliest film," in a 1927 *New York Times* review. Wells accused the film of employing every "cliché, platitude, and generalization imaginable about mechanical progress.[3] Regardless of the film's reception in 1927, it has consistently been referenced by the academy as well as by contemporary popular culture as an important text.

The very popular and contemporary Hip Hop artist Janelle Monáe (Robinson) has picked up Lang's *Metropolis* baton and is running with it in the direction of the future. Monáe clearly references Lang with the picture on her *The ArchAndroid* album cover released in April 2010. On the album cover is a picture of Monáe's alter ego Cindi Mayweather (an android) wearing a headpiece that is very reminiscent of Lang's 1927 theatrical release poster of his *Metropolis* film. Monáe's album cover can be read as a futuristic interpretation of Antonio Sant'Elia's Futurist Italian architectural designs. To be sure, Monáe's beautiful bronze skin, deep brown eyes, and supple lips are far from the metallic lifeless image found on Lang's poster, but the visual reference is stark. Monáe is an artist who draws from several diverse sources (musical, literary, and visual), but seems to be invested in the portrayal of the marginalized body regardless of artistic genre. Monáe's female robot/android, Cindi Mayweather, reads as an attempt to consider the imagining of the mechanical humanoid as a metaphor for other marginalized bodies in the present and future. With her android character, Monáe poses critical questions about the employment and construction of sex, class, race, gender, and the identity of humanity in the present and a speculative future.

Monáe has been the subject of several articles and interviews concerned with her contribution to the cultural and literary aesthetic movement known as Afrofuturism. Afrofuturism is a term that was coined by the cultural critic, Mark Dery, in the early 1990s. The term is useful in this discussion because it combines elements of science fiction, historical fiction and non-Western lens to critique the contemporary dilemmas of people of color, but also to revise, interrogate, and re-examine the historical events of the past. In Gillian Andrews' interview entitled "Janelle Monáe turns rhythm and blues into science fiction," Monáe is very consciously invested in doing more than simply entertaining her audiences with pleasant music.

> Talking about Ray Kurzweil's futurist manifesto, *The Singularity is Near*, it's clear that Monáe is not just a creator of speculative fiction as allegory; she's a futurist. Her music isn't dealing out what-ifs. She's actively trying to prepare us all for what's to come. (*Andrews*)

Monáe is well aware and heavily influenced by science fiction writers like Octavia Butler and Isaac Asimov. Science fiction writers as well as speculative thinkers like Kurzweil are all a part of Monáe's creative process invested in "uniting people with music" (*io9*). I would suggest that Monáe's project transcends the genre of music. Her employment and revision of Lang's robot narrative foreshadows a shift in the way technology and human identity is imagined. Monáe's art allows us to see a direct relationship with the past, present, and the future. Lanre Bakare's article in *The Guardian,* "Afrofuturism Takes Flight: From Sun Ra to Janelle Monáe" appropriately positions Monáe alongside artists such as Octavia Butler, Ishmael Reed, John Sayles (writer/director of *Brother From Another Planet* film), and visual artist Jean-Michel Basquiat.

*ArchAndroid*

Like Butler, Asimov, and Lang, Monáe provides a genesis story for the robot, Cindi Mayweather. The brief narrative can be located in the liner notes of her *ArchAndroid* album cover. True to the genre of science fiction and the form and function of the traditional slave narrative, Monáe's story entails time travel and the validation of her narrative by an authority figure, Max Stelling, Vice Chancellor of The Palace of the Dogs Arts Asylum.[4], [5] According to the research of the Chancellor Stellings, Monae is a time traveler from the year 2719. She was "genoraped and de-existed." Monae was kidnapped by unnamed body snatchers who stole her genetic code and then dislocated her into the past (twenty-first century). Like her African ancestors of the eighteenth and nineteenth century, Monáe was abducted by the equivalent of slavers seeking dark bodies to be sold as chattel in the New World or in her case an Old World. Consequently, Monáe's narrative does not begin with the words "I was born" as does most slave narratives. Instead, her narrative beings with "I will be."

In the year 2719 the genetic thieves sold the genetic code of the displaced Monáe to "the highest bidder at a body farm"(*Chancellor Shellings*). From Monáe's stolen genetic material the biological android, Cindi Mayweather was created. Poetically, the android Mayweather develops into a revolutionary figure self-programmed to free the marginalized citizens of Metropolis from the "Great Divide—a secret society, which has been using time travel to suppress freedom and love throughout the ages" (*Chancellor Shellings*).

The first track on the *ArchAndroid* is "Suite II Overture." The overture serves as an introduction to Monáe's musical narrative. It is appropriately titled because its Romantic era origins are indicative of the work that Monáe's narrative does with the images of marginalized bodies. It is the emotions of the audience that are most important in the rendering of the story of Cindi Mayweather, more so than the facts and dates of the real

Janelle Monáe Robinson. Just as it was with Frederick Douglass' slave narrative, it is the manipulation of the pathos, ethos, and logos of the audience that defines the success of the artistic endeavor. The "Suite II Overture" entails a moment of order for audience and orchestra. The first violin provides a brief tuning note, the audience applauds and orchestra opens abruptly with strings and percussion. The piece begins in earnest with the violins creating a downward cascade of sound that evokes images of impending doom or chaos. As the piece progresses from woodwinds to strings to chorus chant, a contemporary mode is introduced, which evokes images of space and or time travel. The overture ends as abruptly as it began with a cyclone effect caused by strings and percussion, then the applause of the audience. The overture is truly a precursor to the eclectic musical elements that reflect the entire album.

The *ArchAndroid* album was well received by both consumer and music critic. In fact, on its release date in 2010, it made it to number 17 in the US *Billboard 200*, selling 21,000 copies in its first week. Monáe's sophomore album *ArchAndroid* received a Grammy nomination in 2010 for Best Contemporary R&B Album. The populous was and still is very pleased with the images and sounds being produced by Monáe. The point that I would like to emphasize here is that "the monetary investments and yields of this commercial undertaking urgently suggest that America is consciously struggling with the value and employment of dark bodies in its imagination and reality" (Hampton 185). The image of the robot as an allegory for the marginalized citizen is one, if not the most, popular aspect of the *ArchAndroid* album. To be clear, Monáe is a wonderful and creative entertainer who is more than savvy in the African-American musical traditions that she is engaging, but the *hook* that will continue to sell her albums is the speculative fiction that she has written to accompany her singing and dancing. The genius of *ArchAndroid* lies in its ability to veil its subversive attempt to send an empowering message to the marginalized of the present and future. Unlike the evil robot witch of Lang's *Metropolis*, Monae's android is truly a messianic character offering guidance to the Promised Land or Shangri-La. Several critics have lauded Monae's album for its range and musical influence.

> The *ArchAndroid* veers all over the place—ranging from "Wondaland," which describes the whimsical, artificial reality of the same title that Monáe has created for herself and her creative team; "Overtures," influenced by Walt Disney with "symphonies, strings and horns"; "Dance or Die," a Fela Kuti-inspired track featuring Saul Williams; and "Cold War," which Monáe says "reveals what the ArchAndroid looks like." (Concepcion 29)

Cindy Filipenko describes the *ArchAndroid* album as "an ambitious 18-track song cycle she [Monáe] conceived while watching Fritz Lang's cinematic magnum opus *Metropolis*" (Filipenko 36). I am in agreement with most of what the critics say about Monáe's album, but would like to add that *ArchAndroid* can be read or enjoyed as a revolutionary manifesto or a call for an android aesthetic. This manifesto is most clearly articulated in the following three tracks from the *ArchAndroid* album: "Cold War," Tightrope," and "Neon Gumbo."

In the first stanza of "Cold War" the persona of the song informs its audience that a cold war is in effect and that the sanity of the audience may be in jeopardy if sides and objectives are unclear. A cold war is a state of political hostility between countries characterized by threats, propaganda, and other measures short of open warfare, in particular. Given that the persona of the song represents the voice of the android, Cindi Mayweather, the hostility that is implied is not among countries but slave and master or robot and human. The question of "Do you know what you're fighting for?" is used as a refrain throughout the song as a reminder of the urgency of message that is being disseminated. Freedom and the escape from evil and depravity are the goals of Mayweather's cold war. The stigma of moral corruption has been attached to the identity of the marginalized body by the propaganda of the dominant aesthetic and Mayweather wishes to discard such programing. It is the subversive and institutionalized oppression of the persona and those like her that the song attempts to bring to light. Finally, the persona in the song states that ultimately it is peace that is preferred rather than a continued battle of propaganda.

> I'm trying to find my peace
> I was made to believe there's something wrong with me
> And it hurts my heart . . . (25–27)

Despite the fact that the persona has been taught/programed to believe that "there is something wrong with her" and those like her, she seeks freedom from the heart wrenching deceptions of cold war propaganda. In very much the same way as Larry Neal and Maulana Karenga spoke out again an oppressive European/Western aesthetic in their 1968 articles "Black Arts Movement" and "Black Art: Mute Matter Given Force and Function," respectively, Monáe uses "Cold War" to protest against a remaining Western aesthetic that would have marginalized characters (human and robot) believe that there is something wrong with them because they are different from the dominant notion of "normative." Consequently, "Cold War" is a call to consciousness that seeks to make evident the state of warfare despite the lack of overt acts of war.

The song "Tightrope" featuring Big Boi continues towards a trajectory of revolution and resistance. "Tightrope" is a song that provides uplift to the masses of oppressed and marginalized bodies. On its surface it presents a cautionary narrative that warns folks to maintain a sense of balance in their lives as they pursue their goals. Upon closer analysis the tightrope that the persona of the song is referring to might be understood to be a path of a marginalized character away from oppression and towards a state of independence and freedom.

> When you get elevated,
> They love it or they hate it
> You dance up on them haters (13–15)

The "they" that hate the elevation of the marginalized often attempt to prevent the success of the upwardly mobile because of petty prejudices or base jealousy. "They" might take the form of government officials, religious leaders, law enforcers, vigilante organizations or everyday conservative thinking individuals who would rather maintain the status quo instead of supporting radical changes in social order or aesthetics. Whatever the reason might be, the Mayweather persona is clear in her declaration that such obstacle cannot be allowed. The Mayweather persona seems to be insisting that regardless of your status in life, you must continue on the path toward revolution and or freedom for the greater good. The tightrope or path toward freedom is not something that can be avoided.

According to Mayweather's persona, the robot or slave has no other option, if freedom is desired. The message to the masses is that they can choose to follow or lead but they must participate in the revolution or they [the machine] will continue to be blamed for the faults of society as well as remain painted with the signs of immorality and evil. Mayweather is unable to simply complain about the condition of the machine when she is able to "just keep dancing on it."

It is the notion of "dancing on it" that is taken up in Monáe's "Tightrope" video that is especially insightful. The video was released in March of 2010, soon after the *ArchAndroid* album. Tightrope was directed by Wendy Morgan but seems to be in conversation with an experimental short film from 1943 by Maya Deren, entitled *Meshes of the Afternoon*.[6] The short film and contemporary video seem to hinge on questions of sanity. In the asylum that houses the Tightrope video, dancing is forbidden, as it has been known to lead to unlawful magical practices. As stated earlier in this meditation technology has often been mistaken for magic by the unaware and unconscious. This is to say that the dancing that occurs in the video can either be seen as magic or mechanical movement that defies the laws of physics and human movement. There are no obvious images of technology or robots in the "Tightrope" video. The genre of science fiction is not one that would immediately be associated with the narrative that ensues. In fact, the video seems to take place in a very low-tech building that evokes images of poorly administrated health facilities of the early twentieth Century. It is the dancing that places the narrative within the realm of science fiction. And it is the movement of the marginalized bodies in the video that evokes images that might be associated with machines. The tightrope dance entails a gliding that is analogous to hovering across floors and tables by Cindi Mayweather and her equally agile entourage.[7] The dance necessitates a mechanical control of the body that evokes images of super-humans or androids moving to poly-rhythmic baselines that conflate an African past with African American present.

Track number 8 entitled "Neon Gumbo" is Monáe's most blatant call for a musical and Cultural Revolution despite an attempt to hide its message by recording the track on the *ArchAndroid* album backwards. When played in reverse the lyrics are quite clear in their political agenda.

> And when the world just treats you wrong
> Just come with me and I'll take you home
> No need to pack a bag (1–3)

The persona of the song takes on the role of a Harriet Tubman of sorts. The songs reads as though it were a personal message to any mistreated machine or marginalized character in need of a rescue. The persona clearly references the permanence of chattel slavery in referencing the cycle of life spent in servitude from birth to death. When the old man of the house dies his children/babies will continue the oppressive institution of servitude that cannot be survived with patience and perseverance or "from hanging on." "Neon Gumbo" is an urgent appeal to the oppressed machine to immediately exit their current situation and change their life. The persona of the song, Cindi Mayweather, promises to take the oppressed listener home to a Promised Land called Shangri-La.[8] The messianic nature of the "Neon Gumbo" is truly written in neon letters as a message that overtly protests the state of the marginalized. The imagery employed in the song also makes direct references to the institution of American chattel slavery and the subversive and overt practices of runaway slaves seeking freedom and humanity. The fact that the song is recorded backward as though it were written or spoken in a different language is a clear footnote to the coded slave songs of Antebellum America. Not surprisingly, the code-breaking device for Mayweather's message is technological literacy or, at the least, access to the Internet. Regardless of the method used to decipher the message, it is one meant for the minds and hearts of the machines/slaves and not their vaguely curious owners.

Janelle Monáe's employment of the robot motif acts as evidence that popular culture has embraced the inevitable dissemination of humanoid robots and artificial intelligence into mainstream society as a plausible notion. Sadly, the robot's role in popular imagination seems to be limited to a role of chattel and or objectified objects. Notwithstanding this observation, Monáe adroitly demonstrates continuities and discontinuities with images of slaves from the American past and those that will inhabit the American future.

## NOTES

1. *The Birth of a Nation* was silent film released in February 1915 and directed by D.W. Griffith. The film was based on a novel by T. F. Dixon, Jr. entitled, *The Clansman*. The film was the first 12-reel film released in America. Its original release running time was a 133 minutes. In many respects *Birth of a Nation* redefined the possibilities of a cinematic production in the film industry despite its overtly racist content.

2. According to Hebrew mythology, Lilith was the first woman and the first wife of Adam until she escaped from the Garden of Eden.

3. erkelzaar.tsudao.com/reviews/H.G.Wells_on_Metropolis%201927.htm

4. Monáe's validator exists only in her fictional world somewhere in the realm of Hip Hop and the imaginations of her predecessors OutKast, George Clinton, and Sun Ra, but the gesture to the genres of slave narratives and robot novels is smartly done.

5. Palace of the Dogs, which is a fictional place where many great artists have studied, from Jimi Hendrix to Prince and Miles Davis" Monáe says. "Dancing is forbidden there because it leads to magical powers that are illegal" (Concepcion 29). The Palace of the Dogs is a mythical insane asylum where the music video for "Tightrope" track video was filmed,

6. The plot of *Meshes of the Afternoon is as follows:* A woman sees someone on the street as she is walking back to her home. She goes to her room and sleeps on a chair. Monáe's video begins in a room with a bed. Monáe's room is in an insane asylum called The Palace of the Dogs. As soon as Deren's protagonist is asleep, she experiences a dream in which she repeatedly tries to chase a mysterious hooded figure with a mirror for a face but is unable to catch it. The hooded characters are on at margins of Monáe's video. With each failure, she re-enters her house and sees numerous household objects including a key, a knife, a flower, a telephone and a phonograph. The woman follows the hooded figure to her bedroom where she sees the figure hide the knife under a pillow. Throughout the story, she sees multiple instances of herself, all bits of her dream that she has already experienced. The woman tries to kill her sleeping body with a knife but is awakened by a man. The man in Monáe's version of the narrative might be read as Big Boi. The man leads her to the bedroom and she realizes that everything she saw in the dream was actually happening. She notices that the man's posture is similar to that of the hooded figure when it hid the knife under the pillow. She attempts to injure him and fails. Towards the end, the man walks into the house and sees a broken mirror being dropped onto wet ground. He then sees the woman in the chair, who was previously sleeping, but is now dead.

7. The Tightrope dance is very reminiscent to the dance moves popularized by entertainers such as Cab Callaway in the 1930s, James Brown in the 1950s, and Michael Jackson in the 1980s.

8. Shangri-La has is a fictional location that has become synonymous with any earthly paradise. The persona singing "Neon Gumbo" suggests that Shangri-La would be equivalent to a utopian society or a heaven for oppressed robots or slaves.

## REFERENCES

Andrews, Gillian 'Gus'. "Janelle Monáe turns rhythm and blues into science fiction." http://io9.com/5592174/janelle-monae-turns-rhythm-and-blues-into-science-fiction

Bakare, Lanre. "Afrofuturism Takes Flight: From Sun Ra to Janelle Monae." *The Guardian.* http://www.theguardian.com/music/2014/jul/24/space-is-the-place-flying-lotus-janelle-monae-afrofuturism.

Concepcion, Mariel. "Janelle Monae: Rebel Girl." *Billboard Magazine.* 5/1/2010 Vol. 122 Issue 17 p. 29–29. 1p.

Filipenko, Cindy. "Janelle Monáe: The ArchAndroid." *Herozons.* Summer 2011, Vol. 25 Issue 1, p. 36–36.

Hampton, Gregory Jerome. "Imagining Black Bodies in the Future." Found in *Blast, Corrupt, Dismantle, Erase: Contemporary North American Dystopian Literature*. Edited by Brett Josef Grubisic, Gisele M. Baxter, and Tara Lee. (Ontario, Canada: Wilfrid Laurier University Press, 2014), pgs. 181–192.

Minden, Michael. "Fritz Lang's *Metropolis* and the United States." *German Life and Letters* Vol. 53, Issue 3, July 2000, pgs. 340–350.

Monáe, Janelle. *The ArchAndroid*. Released April 2010, Recorded 2008–10 by Wondaland Studios, Atlanta. Label Wondaland Arts Society.

Nama, Adilifu. *Black Space: Imagining Race in Science Fiction Film*. (Austin, Texas: University of Texas Press, 2008.)

Rousseau, Jean-Jacques. *On the Social Contract, Discourse on the Origin of Inequality, Discourse on Political Economy*. Translated and Edited by Donald A. Cress. (Indianapolis, Indiana: Hackett Publishing Company, 1983).

# Conclusion

## *When the Revolution Comes*

In the 1960s artists, poets, and activists cautioned the American public about a revolution that was coming; a revolution that would not be televised and could not be avoided because it had already begun. This revolution threatened to bring necessary social change like a tsunami, leaving nothing in its path that was not new and beautiful according to the black aesthetic that caused its first ripples. According to a few,[1] the revolution entailed a new way of seeing the world around us. The revolution was to be an artistic and philosophical shift founded on a black aesthetic that required all art to be functional, committed, and collective. In theory, if art did not follow these three laws in content and purpose, it was invalid and ultimately counter revolutionary. Arguably, the purifying waters of the Black Arts Movement did not quite yield the change that its rhetoric promised. To be sure, the movement did bring changes and questions regarding the construction of race, class, and gender in the imaginations of the American populous, but the radical change traditionally connoted with revolution did not manifest itself. To the best of my knowledge, there were no violent race riots or civil wars in the streets of American cities because of a call-to-arms by a black aesthetic. The point that I would like to make here is that the robot revolution will not entail a violent and sudden change in our world. Revolutionary change in America is progressive and dependent upon necessity; it is dependent upon rhetoric and the tools of mass media control; and most importantly revolutionary change is sustained by popular consensus.

When the revolution comes, we will lie to ourselves about its arrival. Those who are privileged will deny the obvious facts of change because the past is comforting to those possessed of privilege. When the revolution comes we will attempt to rename it in hopes to control its velocity, trajectory, and affect. We will create art and propaganda to mute the stark contrasts from the past but in time we will accept, adapt, assimilate, and eventually embrace the differences that the revolution will bring. To be sure, society's embrace will not be perfect, loving, or fair. Society's embrace of the coming revolution will not be beautiful, as beauty is understood today; fore it will thrive from a different aesthetic founded on a gaze unsatisfied with yesterday's definition of beauty.

One of the most important points that I would like the readers of this book to consider is that the revolution is not coming because it has already arrived. In fact, the revolution, in whatever form we choose to imagine it, arrived when the notion of change entered our imaginations. The social, political, racial, sexual, and technological revolution is the evolution of human society. How we choose to employ this undeniable fact will dictate how far into the future humanity will be able to travel. Irrational attachments to notions of cultural and biological purity will only function to hinder the evolution of mankind. Homogeneity is a temporary and false unifier that can only end with extinction. By all accounts, homogeneity produces the sort of xenophobia that suffocates the rejuvenating effects of difference. Revolution is the embrace of difference and change that yields survival and growth.

Humanoid robots with artificial intelligence are coming to a household near you and there is nothing to be done about it. Like the flip-up communicators and the handheld electronic tablets used on the warp drive equipped Star Trek Enterprise, robots are either in their infancy or already moving towards their adolescents in terms of development. The cell phone and iPad are firmly located in our imaginations as very real and practical tools to be used everyday of our lives. Robots are the next fantasy to be slated for mundane reality on our quest for a dystopian Republic.

Humanoid robots, like the slaves of antebellum America, will produce significant influences on America's economy, political system, and understanding of racial, sexual, and gender identity. I have provided evidence and discussion that supports the assertion that the robot, like the slave, will be crucial in the reconstruction of the definition of humanity and how it imagines itself. I have employed analysis of literature and film to demonstrate how contemporary society has already begun to produce imagines that meld technology with humanity. The images of robots working with humans found in the media today serve to ease the changes that are forthcoming tomorrow. Broadly speaking, this text demonstrates how robots will irrevocably change our understanding of humanity and its relationship with the technology that it has birthed.

With the creation of a humanoid robotic workforce America will produce a high-tech form of chattel slavery that will undoubtedly produce many, if not all, of the same detrimental effects created by American chattel slavery. The human labor force will have to adapt by improving their technological skills as well as levels of general education. A person's ability to work with various forms of technology will become a nonnegotiable requirement for the common member of the American workforce. It is safe to assume that initially human unemployment rates will reach all-time highs in industries becoming most dependent on robotic labor. Industries dependent on automated production will be the first to benefit significantly from the presence of the humanoid robot. As a result the economy will see advantages and will respond with increases in production and wealth. As AI develops and becomes more advanced, industries that require more human interaction will make greater investment in robot labor. Ultimately, the production cost of a robot will decrease and the domestic robot will become normative and robot/human relations will truly begin to be tested. The new slavery (techno-slavery) will function as a wedge issue for labor movements of tomorrow. Techno-slavery will force human society to consider how much of its humanity it will forego in order to sustain its standard of living and rate of technological advancement. This route of human evolution will undoubtedly disappoint many people, while simultaneously allowing others to revel in the movement toward a utopian republic.

I have acknowledged the trajectory of robotic technology and the coming of AI. My reasoning for drawing parallels between robots and slaves has been two fold. First, as a literary critic and devotee of the late science fiction writer Octavia Butler, I wanted to emphasize the irony in the fact that the genre of science fiction is so lacking in its African-American presence in terms of authorship and audience. And, second, I wanted to demonstrate that the process of systematically or institutionally dehumanizing anything that is distinctly human-like is necessarily detrimental to all parties involved. Regardless of its clever timing and location, propaganda (in the form of cartoons or news reports) that is designed to promote slavery of any sort requires a level of deception on the part of the producer and consumer. If we are to avoid the many potential pitfalls of advanced technologies, we must make great efforts to be honest with ourselves about our desires and our history with slave/master relationships. Phyllis Wheatley reminds us that sin, regardless of its form, can only offer a temporary sweetness that will eventually sink the soul in immense perdition.[2] Let us not repeat the mistakes of the past and be doomed for an eternity.

America's history with the institution of slavery is as significant as its history with institutions of freedom and liberty. The production of robots with artificial intelligence has the potential to yield unimaginable benefits for humanity, but if America is allowed to forget or ignore it's past regressions and hunger for wealth, Terminators are sure to be in its near future. An important point in this book that may not have been articulated as clearly as it should have been is that rhetoric is an extremely powerful weapon, a sword that can be used to save or vanquish a nation. Rhetoric will be the tool used to persuade parents to trust their children with the Robbie and the Mammie of the future. It might also be used to persuade the scientists and robotic engineers of the future to tread with caution and compassion. But most importantly, rhetoric must be used as a tool to disallow the negation of a past that records humanity's great potential for inhumanity.

The hubris of humanity is unbounded when it gazes upon itself in a reflective surface. I have attempted to consider the question of why a man would want to create a machine in his own image. There have been several responses to this query but none so profound as a desire for immortality. Humanity has always been about the work of reproducing and destroying itself. This vocation has entailed the imitation of life on innumerable levels including the production of art and the manipulation of nature. Inbreeding and genocide has loosely framed the spectrum of humanity's activities with eugenics and its quest to wield the powers of creation. But it seems that it will be through technological advances in the area of robotics that will allow humanity to finally gaze upon itself in a reflection of an indefinite future.

As the environmentalists warn us of a deteriorating atmosphere on planet Earth, the robot offers a potential lifeline for humanity. Raymond Kurzweil claims that by the year 2045 humanity will be able to download a human consciousness onto a computer chip.[3] If this becomes a reality, the robot could conceivably equate to the immortality of humanity in the harshest of environments on Earth, or elsewhere. The reasons behind or in front of humanity's choices with regards to technology should be pondered alongside its past. It is only through a lens of the past that a future can be accurately imagined.

## NOTES

1. See "Black Arts Movement" by Larry Neal; "Black Art: Mute Matter Given Force and Function" by Maulana Karenga; and "The Myth of Negro Literature" by Amiri Baraka.

2. See poem "To the University of Cambridge, in New England" by Phillis Wheatley (1753–1784). Poems on Various Subjects. 1773. Lines 29–30.

3. See chapter 1 and Lev Grossman's *Time Magazine* article, "Singularity-2045: The Year Man Becomes Immortal."

# Bibliography

Aldiss, Brian W. *Trillion Year Spree: The History of Science Fiction*. New York: Avon Books, 1986.

Andrews, Gillian 'Gus'. "Janelle Monáe turns rhythm and blues into science fiction." http://io9.com/5592174/janelle-monae-turns-rhythm-and-blues-into-science-fiction

Asimov, Isaac. *I, Robot*. (New York: Doubleday, 1950).

———. *I Asimov: A Memoir*. New York: Random House, 2009.

Bakare, Lanre."Afrofuturism Takes Flight: From Sun Ra to Janelle Monáe." The Guardian. www.theguardian.com/music/2014/jul/24/space-is-the-place-flying-lotus-janelle-monae-afrofuturism.

Bell, Derrick. *Faces at the Bottom of the Well: The Permanence of Racism*, New York: HarperCollins Publishers, 1992.

Bischof, Jackie. "Don't Worry, Get Chappie." Newsweek Global, 00289604, 3/20/2015, Vol. 164, Issue 11.

Blamkamp, Neill. *Chappie*, Columbia Pictures, 2015.

Blassingame, John W. *The Slave Community: Plantation Life in the Antebellum South*. New York: Oxford University Press, 1972.

Bogle, Donald. *Toms, Coon, Mulattoes, Mammies, and Bucks: An Interpretive History of Blacks in American Film, 4th Edition*. New York: Continuum International Publishing, 2001.

Branham, Kristi. "Thrown on Their Own Resources": Collaboration as Survival Strategy in "Imitation of Life." *Literature Film Quarterly*. 2012, Vol. 40 Issue 4, p. 258–273. 16p.

Calvert, Brian. "Slavery in Plato's Republic." The Classical Quarterly, Vol. 37, No. 2 (1987), pp. 367–372.

Capek, Karel. R. U. R. (Rossum's Universal Robots). (London: Penguin Books, 2004).

Carby, Hazel. *Reconstructing Womanhood*. New York: Oxford University Press, 1987.

Chang, Kenneth. "Can Robots Become Conscious," www.nytimes.com/2003/11/11/science/can-robots-become-conscious.html.

Child, Lydia Maria. "The Quadroons." (1842) The Online Archive of Nineteenth-Century U.S. Women's Writings. Ed. Glynis Carr. Online. Internet. Posted: Summer 1997. http://www.facstaff.bucknell.edu/gcarr/19cUSWW/LB/Q.html.

———. "Slavery's Pleasant Homes." (1943) *The Online Archive of Nineteenth-Century U.S. Women's Writings*. Ed. Glynis Carr. Online. Internet. Posted: Summer 1997. www.facstaff.bucknell.edu/gcarr/19cUSWW/LB/SPH.html.

Columbus, Chris. *Bicentennial Man*. Touchstone Pictures/Columbia Pictures/1492 Pictures. 1999.

Concepcion, Mariel. "Janelle Monáe: Rebel Girl." *Billboard Magazine*. 5/1/2010 Vol. 122 Issue 17 p. 29–29. 1p.

Corliss, Richard. "It's Nature vs. Torture in Neill Blomkamp's Chappie." Time.com, 3/10/2015.

Cowper, William. "The Negro's Complaint," http://www.yale.edu/glc/aces/cowper2.htm

Davis, Davis Brion. *The Problem of Slavery in the Age of Emacipation*. New York: Alfred A. Knopf, 2014.

Dick, Philip K. *Do Androids Dream of Electric Sheep?* New York: A Del Rey Book, 1968.

Dixon, Thomas F. Jr. *The Clansman*. Lexington, Kentucky: University of Kentucky Press, 1970.

Douglass, Frederick. *The Narrative of Life of Frederick Douglas*. (Boston: Bedford/St. Martin's, 2003).

———. *Frederick Douglas: The Narrative and Selected Writings*. New York: The Modern Library, 1984.

Dowling, David. "Other and More Terrible Evils": Anticapitalist Rhetoric in Harriet Wilson's Our Nig and Proslavery Propaganda." *College Literature* 36.3 Summer 2009. Pgs. 116–136.

Du Bois, W. E. B. *The Souls of Black Folk*. New York: Bedford/St. Martins, 1997.

———. "The Conservation of Races." www.webdubois.org/dbConsrvOfRaces.html. Posted October 15, 2013.

Farrell, Chris. "Will Robots Create Economic Utopia." www.businessweek.com/articles/2013-02-11/will-robots-create-economic-utopia

Faust, Drew Gilpin, ed *Editor of The Ideology of Slavery: Proslavery Thought in the Antebellum South, 1830–1860*. Louisiana: Louisiana State University Press, 1981.

Fawaz, Ramzi. Book Review. " Super Black: American Pop culture and Black Superheroes/ Do the Gods Wear Capes? Spirituality, Fantasy, and Superheroes/ Race in American Science Fiction." *American Literature*. Mar 2013, Vol. 85 Issue 1, p. 199–202.

Filipenko, Cindy. "Janelle Monáe: The ArchAndroid." Herizons. Summer 2011, Vol. 25 Issue 1, p. 36–36.

Fiesta, Melissa. "Homeplaces in Lydia Maria Child's Abolitionist Rhetoric, 1833–1879." *Rhetoric Review*. 2006, Vol. 25 Vol. 25 Issue 3, p. 260–274.

Flowers, Tiffany A. Book Review. "Race in American Science Fiction." *Western Journal of Black Studies*. Winter 2014, Vol. 38 Issue 4, p. 281–282.

Gong, Li. "The boundary of racial prejudice: Comparing preferences for computer-synthesized White, Black, and robot characters." *Computers in Human Behavior*; Sep. 2008, Vol. 24 Issue 5, p 2074–2093.

Griffith, D. W. *The Birth of a Nation*. David W. Griffith Corp., 1915.

Grossman, Lev. "Singularity-2045: The Year Man Becomes Immortal," *Time Magazine*, http://content.time.com/time/interactive/0,31813,2048601,00.html, Posted February 10, 2011.

Hampton, Gregory Jerome. "Imagining Black Bodies in the Future." Found in *Blast, Corrupt, Dismantle, Erase: Contemporary North American Dystopian Literature*. Edited by Brett Josef Grubisic, Gisele M. Baxter, and Tara Lee. (Ontario, Canada: Wilfrid Laurier University Press, 2014). Pgs. 181–192.

Hanna-Barbera. "Come Home Rosie." *The Jetsons*, Season 2, Episode 2, 1985.

Haraway, Donna. "A Cyborg Manifesto." www.egs.edu/faculty/donna-haraway/articles/donna-haraway-a-cyborg-manifesto/

Harper, Frances E. W. *Iola Leroy*. Boston: Beacon Press, 1987.

Hoppenstand, Gary. "Robots of the Past: Fitz-James O'Brien's "The Wondersmith." *Journal of Popular Culture*, Spring 1994, Vol. 27, Issue 4, pages 13–30.

Hurst, Fannie. *Imitation of Life*. Durham, NC: Duke University Press, 2004.

Jacobs, Harriet. *The Incidents in the Life of Girl*. Cambridge: Harvard University Press, 1987.

Japanese Robot Pop Star video on YouTube posted October 28, 2010. www.youtube.com/watch?v=8LXACLbfRKs.

Jung, C. G. *The Undiscovered Self*. Boston: Little, Brown and Company, 1957.

Kaag, John. "Transgressing the Silence: Lydia Maria Child and the Philosophy of Subversion." *Transactions of the Charles S. Peirce Society*. Winter 2013, Vol. 49 Issue 1, p. 46–53. 8p.

Kiuchi, Yuya. Book Review. "Black Space: Imagining Race in Science Fiction Film by Adilifu Nama." *Journal of American Culture*. Sept 2009, Vol. 32 Issue 3, p. 271–272.

Larsen, Nella. *Quicksand and Passing*. New Brunswick, New Jersey, Rutgers University Press, 1986.

Lavender, Isiah III. *Race in American Science Fiction*. Bloomington: Indiana University Press, 2011.

LeiLani Nishime. "Mulatto Cyborg: Imagining a Multiracial Future." *Cinema Journal* 44, No. 2 Winter 2005. Pg. 34–49.

Levy, David. *Love and Sex with Robots: The Evolution of Human-Robot Relationships.* New York: Harper Collins Publishers, 2007.

Meillassoux, Claude. *The Anthropology of Slavery: The Womb of Iron and Gold.* London and Chicago: Athlone and University of Chicago Press, 1991.

Millett, Paul. "Aristotle and Slavery in Athens." *Greece & Rome, Second Series,* Vol. 54, No. 2 (Oct., 2007), pp. 178–209.

Minden, Michael. "Fritz Lang's Metropolis and the United States." *German Life and Letters* Vol. 53, Issue 3, July 2000, pgs. 340–350.

Monaco, James. *How to Read a Film: Movies Media and Beyond.* New York: Oxford University Press, 2009.

Monáe, Janelle. The ArchAndroid. Released April 2010, Recorded 2008–10 by Wondaland Studios, Atlanta. Label Wondaland Arts Society.

Morrison, Toni, *Playing In the Dark.* Boston: Harvard University Press, 1992.

Nakamura, Miri. "Marking bodily differences: mechanized bodies in Hirabayashi Hatsunosuke's 'Robot' and early Showa robot literature." *Japan Forum,* vol. 19(2) 2007: p 169–190.

Nama, Adilifu. *Black Space: Imagining Race in Science Fiction Film.* Austin, Texas: University of Texas Press, 2008.

Ode, E. V. *The Clockwork Man.* (London: William Heinemann LFD., 1923).

Parrinder, Patrick. "Robots, Clones and Clockwork Men: The Post-Human Perplex in Early Twentieth-Century Literature and Science." *Interdisciplinary Science Reviews,* Vol. 34 No. 1, March, 2009, 56–67.

Perez, Hiram. "Two or Three Spectacular Mulatas and the Queer Pleasures of Overidentification." *Camera Obscura.* Jan 2008, Vol. 23 Issue 67, p. 112–144. 33p.

Piore, Adam. "Friend For Life: Robots Can Already Vacuum Your House and Drive Your Car. Soon, They Will Be Your Companion," *Popular Science,* Vol. 285 No. 5, November 2014. pgs.38–44, 83–84.

Reed, Adolph L. Jr. W. E. B. *Du Bois and American Political Thought: Fabianism and the Color Line.* New York: Oxford University Press, 1997.

Reid Simmons, Maxim Makatchev, Rachel Kirby, Min Kyung Lee, Imran Fanaswala, Brett Browning, Jodi Forlizzi, Majd Sakr, "Believable Robot Characters." *Association for the Advancement of Artificial Intelligence* Winter 2011, pages 39–52.

Richardson, Kathleen. "Mechanical People." *New Scientist;* 6/24/2006, Vol. 190 Issue 2557, p. 56–57.

Robert, Gregg. *Reviews. Social History.* Vol. 25: No. 1, January 2000, pgs. 121–122.

Robertson, Jennifer. "Gendering Humanoid Robots: Robo-Sexism in Japan." *Body and Society;* Jun. 2010, Vol. 16 Issue 2, p. 1–36.

Rousseau, Jean-Jacques. *On the Social Contract, Discourse on the Origin of Inequality, Discourse on Political Economy.* Translated and Edited by Donald A. Cress. (Indianapolis, Indiana: Hackett Publishing Company, 1983).

Scott, Ridley. *Blade Runner.* Warner Brothers. 1982.

Sirk, Douglas. *Imitation of Life.* Universal-International, 1959.

Stahl, John M. *Imitation of Life.* Universal Pictures, 1934.

Strickland, Jonathan. "Could computers and Robots become Conscious? If so, what happens then," science.howstuffworks.com/robot-computer-conscious.htm.

Tatum, Beverly Daniel. Why Are All the Black Kids Sitting Together in the Cafeteria: And Other Conversations About Race. New York: Basic Books, 1997.

Tise, Larry E. Proslavery: A History of the Defense of Slavery in America, 1701–1840. Athens, Georgia: University of Georgia Press, 1987.

Wachowski, Andy and Lana. *The Animatrix* Warner Home Video, 2003.

Walsh, Robert. *An Appeal from the Judgments of Great Britain.* Mitchell, James, and White; William Brown, printed, 1819. New York: Negro Universities Press, 1969.

Washington, Booker T. *Up From Slavery* by Booker T. Washington with Related Documents. New York: Bedford/St. Martins, 2003.

Wheatley, Phillis, "On Being Brought from Africa to America." Found in *Norton Anthology of African American Literature*, edited by Henry Louis Gates Jr., Nellie Y. McKay, New York: W. W. Norton & Company, 2003.

———. "To the University of Cambridge, in New England." Found in Norton Anthology of African American Literature, edited by Henry Louis Gates Jr., Nellie Y. McKay, New York: W. W. Norton & Company, 2003.

Wyman, Joel Howard. Almost Human. Aired from November 17, 2013, through March 3, 2014, on Fox network Television for Frequency Films, Bad Robot Productions and Warner Bros. Television. Fox canceled the series on April 29, 2014.

Yorkin, Nicole. "A Day in the Life: A Family of Four and Their Robots, 25 Years From Now." *Los Angeles Times Magazine*, April 3, 1988. Pgs. 8–23.

# Index

# About the Author

**Gregory Jerome Hampton** holds the title of associate professor of African-American Literature and is the Director of Graduate Studies in the Department of English at Howard University. Dr. Hampton earned his B.A. in Economics and African-American Studies from Oberlin College; an M.A. in African-American Studies from Yale University; and a Ph.D. in Comparative Literature from Duke University. He has published articles in the *English Journal, the CLAJ (College Language Association Journal), Children's Literature in Education: An International Quarterly, Obsidian III,* and *Callaloo.* His most recent courses have been invested in the problematic of the black body and its portrayal in literature and film as well as literature across cultures (African, British, Native American, Caribbean, and Asian). His book *Changing Bodies in the Fiction of Octavia Butler: Slaves, Aliens, and Vampires* (Lexington Books) is the first monograph of literary criticism invested in examining the complete body of fiction produced by Octavia E. Butler. In addition to African-American speculative fiction, Hampton's fields of interest include nineteenth and twentieth century American and African-American literature as well as gender studies.